Parenting With Temperament in Mind is a brilliant, cutting-edge, scientifically informed, and practical caregiver's guide to help you deeply understand your individual child and provide the attuned relational experiences needed to help them thrive. Packed with in-depth explorations of research on the innate temperament that helps shape the emerging personality of our kids, this important book's scientist–parent authors have created a work that combines the best of empirically validated approaches to tailoring our parenting approaches with the effective skills studies have shown to work. Your parenting and your children will be greatly enhanced by soaking in Lengua and Gartstein's practical everyday wisdom.

—**DANIEL J. SIEGEL, MD,** HARVARD MEDICAL SCHOOL, CAMBRIDGE, MA; CLINICAL PROFESSOR OF PSYCHIATRY, UCLA SCHOOL OF MEDICINE, UNIVERSITY OF CALIFORNIA LOS ANGELES (UCLA), LOS ANGELES, CA, UNITED STATES; *NEW YORK TIMES* BESTSELLING AUTHOR, *PERSONALITY AND WHOLENESS IN THERAPY, THE DEVELOPING MIND, PARENTING FROM THE INSIDE OUT,* AND *THE WHOLE BRAIN CHILD*

Lengua and Gartstein have written a most informative guide for parents about how to effectively recognize and address various temperament styles in their young children. Replete with both practical advice and the evidence base underlying their recommendations, these two scientist–practitioners have produced a volume that belongs in every home with young children. Highly recommended!

—**ROBERT J. McMAHON, PhD,** UNIVERSITY OF GEORGIA, ATHENS, GA, UNITED STATES; PROFESSOR EMERITUS AND B.C. LEADERSHIP CHAIR IN REDUCING VIOLENCE AMONG YOUTH, DEPARTMENT OF PSYCHOLOGY, SIMON FRASER UNIVERSITY, VANCOUVER, BRITISH COLUMBIA, CANADA

This book goes well beyond a list of children's temperament traits and ways parents can effectively adapt to their child's traits. The book, by clinical psychologists well known for their research on child development, offers up-to-date insights on the foundations of children's personalities and wise advice on a mindful parenting approach to preventing and managing child behavior problems. Parents who read it will gain richer and more effective ways of being with their children, and clinicians working with families of children with behavior problems will also gain useful ideas from it.

—**JOHN E. BATES, PhD,** PROFESSOR AND DIRECTOR OF CLINICAL TRAINING, DEPARTMENT OF PSYCHOLOGICAL AND BRAIN SCIENCES, INDIANA UNIVERSITY, BLOOMINGTON, IN, UNITED STATES

The authors of this book successfully merge together their expertise as researchers, clinicians, and, as importantly, as parents. The result is a book that makes the scientific foundation of children's temperament accessible to parents and provides numerous practical strategies for parenting children with challenging temperaments.

—**SANDEE McCLOWRY, PhD, RN, FAAN,** UNIVERSITY OF CALIFORNIA, SAN FRANCISCO, CA, UNITED STATES; DEVELOPER OF *NEW INSIGHTS INTO CHILDREN'S TEMPERAMENT*

Written by two well-recognized experts, this book deftly merges the research on temperament and child rearing in a readily accessible way that will enable parents to tailor and personalize an approach that their children will benefit from immensely.

—**DIMITRI A. CHRISTAKIS, MD, MPH;** GEORGE ADKINS PROFESSOR, UNIVERSITY OF WASHINGTON; CHIEF HEALTH OFFICER, SPECIAL OLYMPICS INTERNATIONAL; INVESTIGATOR, CENTER FOR CHILD HEALTH, BEHAVIOR, & DEVELOPMENT, SEATTLE CHILDREN'S RESEARCH INSTITUTE, SEATTLE, WA, UNITED STATES; EDITOR IN CHIEF, *JAMA PEDIATRICS*

Parenting

WITH TEMPERAMENT IN MIND

Parenting WITH TEMPERAMENT IN MIND

NAVIGATING THE CHALLENGES *and* CELEBRATING YOUR CHILD'S STRENGTHS

LILIANA J. LENGUA, *PhD*

MARIA A. GARTSTEIN, *PhD*

AMERICAN PSYCHOLOGICAL ASSOCIATION

Published by
APA LifeTools
750 First Street, NE
Washington, DC 20002
https://www.apa.org

Order Department
https://www.apa.org/pubs/books
order@apa.org

Typeset in Sabon by Circle Graphics, Inc., Reisterstown, MD

Printer: Sheridan Books, Chelsea, MI
Cover Designer: Mark Karis

Library of Congress Cataloging-in-Publication Data

Names: Lengua, Liliana J., author. | Gartstein, Maria A. (Maria Amy), author.
Title: Parenting with temperament in mind : navigating the challenges and celebrating your child's strengths / Liliana J. Lengua, PhD, and Maria A. Gartstein, PhD.
Description: Washington, DC : American Psychological Association, [2024] | Series: APA lifetools series | Includes bibliographical references and index.
Identifiers: LCCN 2023058243 (print) | LCCN 2023058244 (ebook) | ISBN 9781433838606 (paperback) | ISBN 9781433838613 (ebook)
Subjects: LCSH: Parenting—Psychological aspects. | Temperament in children. | Parent and child—Psychological aspects. | BISAC: FAMILY & RELATIONSHIPS / Parenting / General | PSYCHOLOGY / Developmental / Child
Classification: LCC BF723.P25 L446 2024 (print) | LCC BF723.P25 (ebook) | DDC 155.9/24—dc23/eng/20240318
LC record available at https://lccn.loc.gov/2023058243
LC ebook record available at https://lccn.loc.gov/2023058244

https://doi.org/10.1037/0000407-000

Printed in the United States of America

10 9 8 7 6 5 4 3 2 1

This book is dedicated to our families, and especially our children, Natasha, Ariana, Massimo, and Carina, who fundamentally shaped the way we think about temperament and gave us so many opportunities to cultivate humility and empathy as parents and to practice parenting with temperament in mind. We also dedicate this book to the thousands of children and families who participated in our research and other studies that informed this book, making it possible.

CONTENTS

ACKNOWLEDGMENTS

We thank the thousands of children and families who participated in our research and other studies that informed this book, making it possible. We also acknowledge the mentors and collaborators who informed our temperament and child development research, including Mary Rothbart, Nancy Eisenberg, Mark Greenberg, Martha Ann Bell, and Sam Putnam. Our research was made possible by grants from the National Institute of Mental Health, Eunice Kennedy Shriver National Institute of Child Health and Human Development, the National Science Foundation, and the Martiz Family Foundation.

Parenting
WITH TEMPERAMENT IN MIND

INTRODUCTION

TAILORING YOUR PARENTING TO YOUR CHILD'S TEMPERAMENT

Is your child clinging to you at the door when you try to drop them off at a birthday party, too scared to join the party? Or is your child so excited to get to the party that they dart into the street even after you tell them to stay right by the car? Or does your child not even make it to the party because they are so frustrated and angry about having to wear a jacket that they break down into a crying and yelling fit? And do you feel self-conscious that other parents view you as ineffective with our out-of-control child?

Some of these challenging behaviors from our children can stem from their *temperament*—the emotional and self-regulation characteristics that they are born with. Many children present with challenges in their emotional and behavioral responses to everyday situations, and these can be stressful for parents and families. In addition, children with particular temperamental emotion and behavior characteristics can face an increased risk for social, emotional, and behavioral problems, such as anxiety, depression, or oppositional problems, in particular when they experience stress or adversity. These temperament-driven behaviors can be overwhelming to parents who might not know the most effective way to deal with them. Most important, children can present these challenging behaviors for very different underlying reasons depending on their temperament, and parents can be more effective if they understand the source of their children's reactions.

It's not always clear what is the most effective way to deal with these behaviors. Should a parent use more negative consequences? More rewards? Be more firm? More gentle? Pick your battles? Stick to your guns? Sometimes, parents receive conflicting advice that is confusing without a better sense of the temperament characteristics underlying challenging behaviors.

Most parents who have more than one child will tell you that what worked with one didn't necessarily work with the other. They felt like they knew what they were doing—until their second one came along, and nothing worked the same. Or ask parents with one child who just seemed more demanding than their friends' kids were about the experience of receiving their friends' judgments about how "that's what only-kids are like." Little, if any, parenting wisdom or advice that is available to parents provides the critical understanding of the role of children's temperament in shaping children's behavior and our parenting.

We wrote this book to clarify how different temperament characteristics can lead to challenging emotional and behavioral responses from children and to explain how parents can tailor their parenting to better support their children's positive development with different temperament characteristics in mind. We offer specific parenting approaches to address these different temperament characteristics. We hope the book provides important insight and practical suggestions to every parent, giving an understanding of children's temperament, that is, their motivational styles, emotional reactions, self-control, their strengths, and areas that require extra support. The recommendations in this book are most helpful to parents with younger children, infants through grade school ages, although parents with tweens and teens might also benefit from a better understanding of their children's emotional reactions, motivations, and ability to self-regulate.

We begin the book by defining and describing children's temperament using the most current research perspectives based on our own work and studies conducted by leading experts in the field. We provide information about the underlying neurobiological systems so that parents can have a better understanding of how children's motivational and emotional tendencies drive their behaviors. By understanding the neurobiological systems underlying the behaviors and physiology–behavior relationships, parents can gain a broader perspective and develop more empathy for the behaviors as well as gain a better understanding of how to effectively address them. We then lay out how specific temperament characteristics can lead parents to react in particular ways to their children and how their children might react differently to parenting. We focus on the temperament characteristics that have been shown to pose challenges for parents or that are related to increased likelihood of social, emotional, or behavioral problems in children. The focus is on how parents can support children's positive development and work most effectively with their children to promote their well-being.

ABOUT US

Throughout this book, we use the first-person singular voice ("I") whenever one of us is relating an example from her own personal or professional life. We will clarify who is speaking when we do this.

Liliana J. Lengua

I (Liliana) am a University of Washington professor of psychology and the founding director of the Center for Child and Family Well-Being. I conduct research on how children and parents react differently to each other on the basis of children's temperament characteristics, as well as how parents can support their children's unique characteristics while also shaping them into strengths and positive social–emotional outcomes. I also study how children's temperament contributes to their social, emotional, and behavioral adjustment in response to stress and adversity. In addition, I am a clinical psychologist, and in community workshops and my past practice I have worked to help parents be more effective by facilitating their understanding of their children's unique motivations and emotional reactions. I have published more than 150 scholarly articles and chapters on temperament; parenting; and children's social, emotional, and behavioral responses to stress and adversity. Finally, I am a mother of three children, each with a unique temperament profile and each presenting his or her own challenges, insights, cherished qualities, and engaging stories of parenting experiences. I call them my "temperament lab at home."

When my oldest child was born, she didn't cry or make a sound for a couple of minutes. When the doctor handed her to me, she looked stunned. Her eyes were wide saucers, her neck stretched out, and her head turned side to side. And then she started to wail. She cried and arched her back and flailed. The nurse encouraged me to try breastfeeding her, but she arched away and turned her head. My husband took her and tried to walk around with her, holding her close to his chest. After several minutes of trying, he tried putting a pacifier in her mouth, as the nurse suggested. After that didn't work, a nurse tried soothing her.

My daughter continued to cry, with each nurse on that shift coming in to take her turn at trying to calm her. I tried breastfeeding again. Another nurse tried giving her a bit of sugar; another tried swaddling her. She was going on an hour of crying at the point when there was a shift change, and all the new nurses on the next shift tried their tricks for soothing infants. Finally, after almost two hours straight of inconsolable crying, a nurse brought in a tub of warm water and held her in it. She finally quieted, and afterward nursed and let me, and then my husband, hold her as she slept.

Because of my research experience on children's temperament, I knew this was a sign that my daughter was probably going to be a reactive child. But even though I knew about this aspect of her temperament, I did not have very specific guidance about what I should do differently or how I could effectively respond to my daughter's reactivity. In fact, even as research on the interplay between parenting and children's temperament has burgeoned in the past 40 years, very little of that research has been translated into meaningful guidance for parents about how to effectively interact with their children who have different temperament characteristics. Until recently, if you did a web search on the term "temperament," you were more likely to find information about the temperament of dogs and horses than about children. Even today, most of the information available to parents is based on a model of temperament that was developed in the 1950s.

Although my daughter's temperament made some things challenging, it also made some things easier, like teaching her about dangers to avoid or getting her to follow rules and expectations, and her reactivity helped her grow into a conscientious, responsible teen who was passionate about social issues and cared deeply about her siblings and friends.

My second child was equally challenging, but in a way that was entirely different from his older sister. Mind you, I thought I had had my temperamental child in my first one. I didn't think it was statistically likely that I would have a second one, let alone one who was completely different! I thought that, given the genetics of temperament, I would be likely to have another child who was challenging in similar ways. I did not expect to be challenged in the ways my son presented. It was like learning parenting all over again, trying to figure out what would be effective with my son, because most of the things I did with my daughter weren't working as well with him.

My third child was much more composed and calm, soothable, and easygoing. However, she was often very persistent and inflexible, and she presented different challenges that raising two children already hadn't provided insights about.

Let me say at the outset that I treasure each of my children deeply, and there is (almost) nothing I would change about any of them. In fact, my "temperament lab at home" provided me with tremendous insight into parenting, which has informed my research and provided me with greater humility and compassion in this parenting endeavor we undertake. But I never dreamed what a wild ride it would be to have three dramatically different children, and I was not prepared for how differently I had to parent each of them. Keep in mind that I'm a child psychologist, who researches temperament and has substantial knowledge about parenting, and even I wasn't ready for it.

Maria A. Gartstein

I (Maria, or "Masha") am a Washington State University professor and chair of the psychology department. I am a clinical psychologist who specializes in work with children and families in my practice and supervision and a developmental scientist in my laboratory. My research focuses on early childhood temperament and how these emerging traits are related to parenting and the ways in which caregivers interact with young children. I have focused on both biological and environmental factors that play a role in how children's unique characteristics develop, and I have conducted studies that focused on so-called "child effects," increasing our understanding of how children's temperament shapes parenting and caregiving they receive. Because of this work, I was asked to contribute to a Netflix documentary titled "Babies," specifically, the episode titled "Nature and Nurture." I have authored more than 100 peer-reviewed scholarly publications, along with book chapters and scientific presentations. As a parent, I have faced a number of temperament-related challenges, which provided further insights I am eager to share with parents and providers who work with children and families.

My story of translating scientific knowledge about temperament into parenting differs in details from Liliana's but also shares a common theme—A long-standing program of temperament research did not prepare me fully for challenges of my own child's temperament. I had my daughter later in life, thinking that all of the scientific knowledge I was able to gain pursuing a concentrated study of how temperament develops, what combination of nature and nurture shapes this development, and how it ultimately contributes to risk or protects the child from maladjustment and mental health issues would give me an advantage. When my daughter and I just met each other and were still in the hospital, I was pleased to hear all of the nurses comment on how alert she was. I thought it would be great to have a child so interested in what was going on in the world around her. As she grew, this interest turned into a lot of activity, pursuing different things that seemed to promise a reward of some kind. In fact, she skipped crawling altogether, moving right to standing, walking, running, and climbing. One night, I came into her bedroom after hearing her crying to discover that she had pulled herself up to a standing position in her crib and then was not sure how to get back down. I will never forget our first day at a local gymnastics club for their "wiggle worms" class; it was one of the happiest days of my life. For the first time since she had begun walking, running, and climbing, it was safe to let her do all the things she had been wanting to do so badly. I learned that day that one of the biggest challenges for me would be to channel her zest for life, all things interesting and potentially rewarding, in a safe, healthy, and productive direction. This work continues today.

When she became a toddler, being so interested and driven to explore meant that every time we went out for a meal, she wanted to visit the restroom on multiple occasions, leading me to develop a rule: Only two visits to the restroom per restaurant outing. The other rule that quickly became a necessity was "When I say it's time to go, it's time to go!" There were definitely a few times when she tested this rule, with me carrying her out of play areas and other locations and other parents looking at me with judgment in their eyes, but over time we began to understand each other. Being consistent in setting this limit ultimately paid off, and one day at a playground we called the "big kids' slide" she said, "I know, I know. . . . When it's time to go, it's time to go." I also learned that sometimes I had to back away from rules and limitations, because enforcing them meant I ended up feeling very bad about being a parent. One time, a misbehavior led me to say to my daughter that if she was not able to follow my instruction on the third time it was given, she would not be going to a friend's birthday party. You can probably anticipate how this ended: She did not go to the party, and I had to call the birthday girl's parents and apologize, which left me feeling like the worst mother ever. This situation resulted in me deciding I would avoid power struggles before important events, even if it meant compromising on things I normally would not. I can share many similar examples, and our relationship is still a work in progress. However, this foundation, which mixed consistency with flexibility on my part, gave us a solid start.

SHARING TEMPERAMENT INSIGHTS WITH PARENTS

In the 1950s, Alexander Thomas and Stella Chess (1977) conducted a small but groundbreaking study on infant temperament. At that time, the overwhelming consensus was that all of our behavior, everything we do and who we are, was the result of *nurture*, learned starting in infancy. This behaviorist perspective indicated that we became who we are through imitation, modeling, socialization, and living through experiences. Thomas and Chess put a crack in that perspective when they interviewed parents of infants and discovered notable differences in infant sleep and eating patterns, crying frequency and intensity, soothability, sensitivity, adaptability, and flexibility to changes around them. Thomas and Chess put something new on the table—the notion that children come into the world with individual differences in certain characteristics, that is, *nature*—and that parents respond differently to children depending on their temperament. For the next 30 years, research on children's temperament and the role it plays in parenting and in children's social, emotional, and behavioral well-being grew, chipping away at prior conceptions that all of these individual differences were the result of nurture, or learning.

Then, in the 1980s, new research by Mary Rothbart (2007) advanced our understanding of children's temperament by linking observed individual differences to neurobiological systems that might account for them and fine-tuning our understanding of how these underlying systems lead to individual differences in children's reactions to their environment and experiences. Unfortunately, information stemming from this refined model has not yet reached parents or been made accessible as useful information to guide parenting children with different, and sometimes challenging, temperament characteristics. This is our primary goal in this book.

In this book, we share research-based knowledge about children's temperament and how it leads children to respond uniquely to parenting efforts as validated through clinical and personal experiences. We provide a summary of the most current understanding of children's temperament, the biological systems and physiological processes that underlie important differences in children's perspectives of and reactions to the world, their motivations and drives in different situations, and their capacity to modulate or manage their own reactions. We share recommendations based on the findings of the past 40 years of research that provide insight into how parents respond differently to different temperament characteristics in their children and what parenting behaviors work best for which children.

Most important, we offer suggestions for parenting strategies that work best at guiding our temperamentally challenging children to more adaptive pathways over time, at different points in their development. Our ultimate hope is to provide parents tools to help them to be effective in responding to their children's sometimes challenging, sometimes frustrating, sometimes heartbreaking, often endearing, delightful, puzzling, overwhelming, and enjoyable behaviors so that parents can be more effective in raising socially, emotionally, and behaviorally well-adjusted children.

HOW THIS BOOK IS ORGANIZED

In Part I of this book we introduce definitions of temperament and parenting behaviors that we discuss throughout the book. We start with a description of what temperament is (Chapter 1), the behaviors associated with different temperament characteristics (Chapter 2), and the biological systems that are the basis for children's temperament (Chapter 3). We then introduce the four core parenting principles that are most often associated with children's positive development and well-being (Chapter 4).

In Part II, we discuss the temperament characteristics that, when very strong, can present challenges related to children's social, emotional, and behavioral development and well-being. These include being very fearful or very fearless (Chapter 5), easily frustrated (Chapter 6), impulsive (Chapter 7), and inflexible (Chapter 8). We explore how these characteristics are experienced by parents and discuss which parenting behaviors tend to be effective with each particular temperament characteristic.

In Part III, we offer a toolkit of parenting practices that allow parents to be more responsive to and effective with their children's temperament. This includes practices for being present (Chapter 9), being warm (Chapter 10), being balanced (Chapter 11), and being consistent (Chapters 12 and 13). You might think of this book as being like a cookbook, where Part II gives broad advice on how to cook (or, in our case, how to parent) and Part III provides specific recipes (or, in our case, specific practices and exercises). Throughout the chapters in Part II, we refer you to the tools described in Part III. You might find yourself going back and forth between chapters in Parts II and III. We invite you to read the book out of order, if you find that useful, and to try out some of the parenting practices as you read through the chapters in Part II.

Finally, in our appendixes we offer questionnaires to help you assess your own family situation. Appendix A will help you evaluate your child's temperament characteristics, and Appendix B will help you evaluate your own parenting in terms of the core parenting principles presented in this book. We provide these temperament and parenting assessment tools in part because, in our work with families, parents routinely express an interest in being able to benchmark their own efforts, and they have often told us how responding to questions about child temperament made them better observers of their children's behaviors and increased their appreciation of their meaning. We invite you to use the information about temperament in Parts I and II, the parenting practices in Part III, and the questionnaires in the Appendices in ways that are most helpful for enhancing your enjoyment of your child and effectiveness in supporting your child's positive development and well-being.

I

UNDERSTANDING TEMPERAMENT AND PARENTING

CHAPTER 1

WHAT IS TEMPERAMENT?

Who would have thought that an electric outlet—well, not the outlet itself, but one's relationship with it—could be so telling? One day, when my (Liliana's) oldest was starting to crawl about independently, around the age of 6 months, she approached an electric outlet. Of course, we had most of our outlets babyproofed. But there were things plugged into the wall, like a lamp and a baby monitor, that held some allure to her. As she reached for the plug, I said, with some urgency, "Oh, no. No touching. Ouchy. No touching." My daughter looked up at me, a bit stunned, then back at the outlet, looking quite shaken. Maybe I laid it on too thick, but I was using *threat signaling*—providing a cue of a potential danger—to teach her to stay away. I picked her up and comforted her, and we found something else to play with. I honestly can't remember her ever trying to touch an outlet or plug again. Actually, when she was older, I had to nudge her to try to plug something in and had to encourage her so that she wouldn't be afraid to do it. Talk about one-trial learning!

When my middle child was around the same age, he and I had a nearly identical interaction. As he reached for the plug, I responded with, "No, no. Ouchy, no touching." He seemed annoyed. He was seriously interested in figuring out that outlet, and truly no degree of warning, countless removals, and efforts to distract, or endless repetitions of "no, no," had any effect on his daily efforts to touch the outlets. In fact, one day as I was in his room selecting a new post–poop-leaking-out-of-the-diaper outfit, he was on the floor making a beeline to the monitor plug. He managed to slip his tiny finger between the plug and the outlet such that the plug was still engaged. I turned just in time to see him shudder (presumably from an electric charge), fall back, look at his finger, look at the plug, make a sound that sounded a bit like a pirate's "Aargh" and, remarkably, again reach for the plug. There were very few one-trial, threat-signaling learning experiences with my son when he was young.

My children's early relationships with the electric outlets in our house were indeed telling of their reactions to their experiences; of how they respond differently to threats, challenges, and rewards; of their relationships with people in their lives; and of the very fundamental, core aspects of their personality: their temperament. Temperament differences play a central role in how our children react to us as their parents, how we react to our children, and the trajectories we are able to set our children on as they grow into the independence of later childhood and adolescence.

In this chapter, we define temperament, sharing a little about some traditional perspectives, and then providing a contemporary understanding of it. We introduce what temperament behaviors look like and where they come from. We then discuss how temperament might affect parenting and children's well-being, elaborating on this for the specific temperament characteristics we address in Part II of the book.

REACTIVITY AND REGULATION

People use the term *temperament* to mean a lot of different things, but it generally refers to characteristics that a person was born with, that are inherent to that person's makeup in some way, and that are consistent over time when a person is in particular situations. In ancient medicine and philosophical perspectives, such as the Indian Ayurveda system of medicine and the Greek and Roman physicians and philosophers, our temperament was determined by the balance of four body fluids, or *humors*. A relative preponderance of phlegm made one *phlegmatic*: relaxed or peaceful, but possibly apathetic. A *sanguine* person was one with excess blood, an individual who was optimistic and social, perhaps passionate. A person with a greater presence of black bile was *melancholic*, analytic or quiet but also possibly depressive, and a person with a greater degree of yellow bile, labeled *choleric*, was thought to be short-tempered and irritable.

Although our understanding of neurobiological systems and functioning has advanced since these perspectives on temperament were held, these ancient understandings of the ways in which individuals differed fundamentally might not have been too far off. In contemporary approaches to temperament, we think of individuals as differing in how emotionally reactive they are to experiences or how introverted or extroverted they are, that is, how social they are. Temperament is not exclusive to humans, and when we talk about the temperament of an animal, such as a horse or dog, we think of how energetic, sensitive, responsive, stubborn, "emotional," or reactive the animal is. Most of these approaches converge around basic emotions and motivations, the things that drive us, things that appeal to us, and how we react to our experiences.

In contemporary approaches, temperament is defined as comprising biologically based individual differences in reactivity and regulation (Rothbart, 2007; Rothbart & Bates, 2006). These include motivation, affect or emotion, activity or energy level, attention, and behavioral control characteristics. *Reactivity* refers to how an individual responds to change in their environment or experience, including physiological arousal and emotional reactions. People can differ in how quickly and intensely they react and the typical kind of emotional reaction they experience. We can see individual differences in reactivity early in life, immediately after birth and, studies suggest, even in utero. When discussing *temperament reactivity*, we are usually referring to expressions of the most basic emotions and behaviors driven by motivation systems. These commonly include arousal of frustration or anger, fear (inhibition, withdrawal), approach, and pleasure or delight. Most of us can think of someone whose first reaction to a new situation or person is to be worried, inhibited, or cautious; conversely, we all probably know another person whose first reaction is excitement and approach, sometimes without really thinking about the implications or consequences of this behavior. In this sense, temperament reactivity refers to a person's most common or typical basic emotional or physiological response to particular situations or experiences. There is also an information-processing layer to temperament that involves sensitivity to different experiences. For example, a fearful child who hesitates to seek out new experiences can be described as particularly sensitive to potential threat and danger, prioritizing this information in their decisions. This, in turn, makes them sensitive to novelty or uncertainty, reacting with fearfulness and avoidance. Given the biological basis of temperament, it should not be a surprise that temperament tendencies can also be understood with respect to underlying brain activity and physiological profiles, such as heart rate variability or stress hormone (cortisol) concentrations. We will say more about this in Chapter 3 to provide a more complete understanding of how these emotional and motivational systems work.

Before I (Liliana) had my own children, I did what most people probably do and thought that most of the behaviors I observed in other people's children were a result of how they parented their children. As a temperament researcher, I knew that was only partly true, but I still had a bias toward thinking that children behaved in ways that their parents socialized them to behave. But as my friends started having children, I started paying attention to the differences in their children's reactions to everyday events.

One evening, I was visiting a friend whose 18-month-old daughter, Michele, was playing in the kitchen while we were in there talking. Michele was walking along the floor when she suddenly froze, shaking, with a look of terror on her face, and then started to cry. Her mother ran over to pick her up and comfort her. I was completely baffled. I had no clue as to what Michele was afraid of until her mom pointed out a drop of water on the tile floor. She explained that just the day before, Michele had slipped and fallen on a puddle of water that was on the floor, and feeling the water under her foot had sent her into a panic.

Another time, I was visiting other friends who had a daughter, Sara, who was also about 18 months old. While her parents sat on the couch talking with my husband and me, Sara was climbing all over the couch. She crawled like a cat from one arm of the couch, over the back, to the other arm, where a throw blanket hung. It occurred to me about a second before it happened that if she crawled onto the blanket hanging over the arm of the couch, both she and the blanket were likely to slip and fall—which is exactly what happened. Sara landed with a thud on the hardwood floors flat on her back, stared at the ceiling for a moment or two, and broke out in a delighted squeal. She went on to ride the blanket off the arm of the couch over and over again, laughing the whole time. Michele's and Sara's individual reactions to similar events point to core differences in how children experience and react to situations and events and highlight individual differences in basic emotional reactions, such as fear or delight.

Temperament self-regulation, or sometimes called *effortful control*, refers to the orienting, focusing, and shifting of attention and control of behavior that serve to change the level of reactivity, either increasing an emotion or motivation that facilitates what we are trying to achieve or reducing or inhibiting an emotion or motivation that is counterproductive to achieving a goal. We can think of it as how efficiently and effectively we can recover from or reduce our arousal, increase our motivation as needed, or manage our behaviors to fit a situation. *Self-regulation* includes the things we do to modulate, either decrease or increase, our physiological, emotional, or behavioral response to match the demands of a situation. In one situation, we might need to ratchet down our anger to get through a meeting at work more effectively, and in another situation we might need to amp up our energy to make ourselves do something we don't really want to do, like exercise. We might accomplish this by focusing on our goal, or paying attention to the desirable aspects of a situation and shifting our focus away from the less desirable aspects. For example, you might be angry in a meeting at work because of something someone says, but by focusing on presenting yourself as professional and calm to others in the meeting you might be able to manage your anger more effectively. If you stay focused on the negative comment that made you angry, you're more likely to remain angry and might not be able to navigate the meeting effectively.

We also self-regulate by inhibiting responses or behaviors that we might be inclined to engage in if we let our emotions drive us. You might not feel like leaving the house at 5:45 in the morning to go running or walking; instead, you might feel like staying in your warm, comfy bed. But to accomplish a goal of staying healthy and fit, you have to suppress the desire to stay in bed, overcome the resistance to going outside in the cold, and make yourself get up and leave the house. You might do this by focusing on how good it feels after you exercise, how important it is to you to have a healthy lifestyle, and building up your self-control to push through your initial resistance. Temperament self-regulation is our inherent individual differences in the capacity to manage emotions and behaviors to match the demands of a particular situation. Over time, we might build self-regulation through means other than our temperament.

However, much of young children's self-regulation is rooted in their temperament.

As an example, my (Liliana) two younger children are both very reward-oriented. When they were little, if there was a plate of cookies on the counter to have for dessert after dinner, they both were pretty excited about the cookies and had a hard time putting them out of their mind until after dinner. However, my son tended to focus on the cookies, looking at them, anticipating how good they would taste, smelling them to whet his appetite, sitting near them as he played, reaching for them jokingly (or not), and asking repeatedly if he could have one now. My daughter would use a different tactic. She would look for ways to put the cookies out of her mind, like distracting herself or playing somewhere else in the house, or she would ask that, if she waits patiently, could she maybe have two cookies instead of one after dinner. And sometimes she would even ask if she could save one of her cookies for the next day instead of eating them both at one time. She was using classic self-control strategies, like inhibiting her initial response, distraction, or planning, to tolerate having to wait for the cookies. Her self-regulation made her more successful in situations like this and less challenging to those around her.

WHERE DOES TEMPERAMENT COME FROM?

In general, we recognize that temperament is genetically based, with somewhere between one-quarter and one-half of our temperament characteristics being inherited genetically, that is, through nature. If your child tends to be more fearful or easily frustrated or impulsive, then there is a pretty good chance there is someone in your child's family—parents, grandparents, aunts or uncles—who also tends to have that characteristic. Sometimes we think our children will be mini-me's—that is, their personality will be like our own—and sometimes that is true, but they can also have characteristics of others.

Our temperament is also pretty stable; that is, we are likely to see consistency in our temperament characteristics over time, although the way the characteristics are expressed might differ as children grow older. Children who are more shy or withdrawn when they are younger are likely to show some shyness later on, and children who are more impulsive when they are younger tend to be more impulsive when they are older, although the nature of that shyness or impulsivity might look different. A child who is shy when he is young might cling to his mother's leg when an adult tries to talk with him. That would be a very strange thing for an adolescent to do, but that shy adolescent might now choose not to go ask a sales clerk a question in a store because he is too timid to do so.

However, there are also substantial portions of our temperament that can be shaped or altered by our experiences. For example, a person who was very shy and withdrawn as a child might overcome his tendency to avoid new or unfamiliar situations or people, learn skills for socializing and interacting that make him more comfortable in new situations, and as a result be less shy, or at least come across as less shy. Most people will indicate that they still feel a bit of anxiety or inhibition in unfamiliar situations, but now they have the tools to handle them more effectively, so they don't let their inhibition stop them. So, temperament might be viewed as an individual's likely or typical response range that makes them more or less likely to react in a particular way to immediate experiences. Being higher in a particular temperament characteristic might lead an individual to select particular experiences that are more comfortable or desirable for that person, or that provide a better fit. However, temperament is also a function of experience, practice, and training, and certain characteristics may be selectively shaped because the context may be more or less accepting or accommodating of the child's characteristic responses. For example, parents and teachers might work diligently on shaping a child's emotional response to a situation if he is typically angry or frustrated, for example, through encouraging and rewarding desired behaviors and providing a consistent routine. In this way, the child can develop tools for regulating those reactions. In Part II, we describe more strategies for supporting children's regulation of their emotions.

To summarize, temperament represents biologically based characteristics that are present early in life, that shape and are shaped within the context of social and environmental interactions and experiences, and that result in different levels of sensitivity and responsiveness to those experiences. Because of this interplay between temperament and experiences throughout development, we can see how integral parents and other adults are to shaping children's temperamental reactivity and self-regulation. This influence begins in infancy through the way we respond to our child's individual reactions, selectively encouraging or discouraging some. At the same time, as we have noted, a child's temperament might lead to our own emotional reactions to them, shaping our responses and parenting. This book should help parents become more mindful of such patterns and using these to help their children become their best selves.

THE ROLE OF PARENTS' TEMPERAMENT

Parents' own temperament can be like a filter of information about their child's reactivity and regulation and can affect how they respond to their child's temperament. For example, a parent who is fearful or anxious may be very sensitive to their child's reaction to novelty and try to protect their child from experiencing anxiety. This can lead to a parent being too accommodating of their child's avoidance and withdrawal from novel but important situations (e.g., a new activity, the birthday party of a new friend). On the other hand, a parent who is easily frustrated might react to the same fearful child with anger or criticism, making what should be a straightforward situation more complicated. A parent who is easily frustrated might also react with strong angry outbursts in response to their child's frustration, leading to an escalation of conflict between them. Really, any significant mismatch between parent and child temperament could lead to challenges. For example, my (Masha's) daughter's high activity level is similar to my husband's temperament, but I tend to move at a slower speed. There was definitely a learning curve for me in trying to figure out how to manage this very active young lady, especially once walking started at around 10 months of age. Insights about different activities, like "wiggle worms" and regular trips to playgrounds with what we affectionately referred to as "big kids' slides," were critical, and I also accepted the reality of having to live with being very tired and maximizing nap time. I also learned that sometimes I needed a break, so starting part-time day care turned out to be an important part of our routine.

Given that a parent's, caregiver's, or teacher's own temperament can influence how they interpret and react to a child's behaviors in a situation, it is useful to parents and other adults in a child's life to reflect on their own temperament and how it plays out in interactions with their children. In Chapter 2 we provide a tool for understanding your child's temperament, and parents can also consider how those descriptions apply to them now or how they applied to them when they were children.

TEMPERAMENT AND STRESS

Temperament alters how individuals respond to stress and adversity on behavioral, emotional, and physiological levels. People who are generally more likely to experience fear or frustration, or who tend to have strong emotional reactions or trouble regulating their emotional reactions, tend to respond to stress more negatively. Research has shown that children who are higher in negative emotionality or lower in self-regulation are more likely to develop emotional or behavioral problems compared with other children when they experience stressful family, school, or social environments (Lengua & Wachs, 2012). For example, when parents or families have high levels of conflict, or the household is disorganized or chaotic, or when a family experiences divorce, children with high negative emotionality or low self-regulation are more likely to show symptoms of depression, anxiety, or aggression. Similarly, when families experience an accumulation of stress or adversity associated with low income or economic hardship, children who tend to be high in negative emotionality more often fare worse, whereas children higher in self-regulation show relatively better adjustment (Lengua & Wachs, 2012). These temperament characteristics can lead children to have heightened perceptions of threat of potential loss or harm when stressors occur, and they might also be less able to problem-solve or cope effectively with the stress.

It is important to remember that our children's responses to stress are not determined entirely by their temperament. A child's temperament profile is one of many factors that contribute to their responses to stress. Some of the other factors include the support they receive from caregivers, family, and friends; the resources a family has to create a stable, predictable environment; and coping tools a child has developed over time. The effects of these other factors give parents (and other caregivers and teachers) the critical opportunity to support their children during stressful times in a way that their temperament requires and that helps them successfully navigate stressful situations. It is our hope that a better understanding of children's temperament can also help families support their children when experiencing stress and adversity.

TEMPERAMENT AND WELL-BEING

The interplay between parenting and temperament is important to our children's well-being. Extensive research shows that temperament is a robust contributor to children's social and emotional development and their behavioral and emotional problems (e.g., Kiff et al., 2011). In Part II of the book we discuss the specific benefits and risks of each temperament characteristic, but in general, some temperament characteristics, such as good self-regulation, contribute to the development of children's social, emotional, and academic competencies, including good social skills, behavioral control, and emotional well-being. Other temperamental characteristics can contribute to problems in those areas. For example, fearful children are more likely to develop anxiety problems, and children who are easily and intensely frustrated in challenging situations may be at risk for developing problems with peers, negative relationships with parents or teachers, aggression, and depression. In this book, we focus on the characteristics that tend to pose challenges for parents or that can increase the likelihood of social, emotional, or behavioral problems, and we provide tools for managing these.

Temperament may have effects on children's adjustment in a number of ways. Some characteristics make it easier for parents and teachers to socialize and support responsible and prosocial behaviors, empathy, and sympathy. Other temperament characteristics directly increase the chance of social and emotional problems, and some temperament effects are more indirect; that is, some temperament characteristics might lead children to choose or structure their experiences in ways that contribute to problems. For example, fearful children might avoid unfamiliar people or situations, so they may become more socially withdrawn over time and have fewer socially enriching experiences. Temperament can also lead to adjustment problems, for example, if a child's reactions to situations consistently elicit particular reactions in others. An impulsive child might frequently blurt out responses in class or rush through their work, so they elicit more negative responses from their teachers, which, over time, can contribute to problems with self-esteem or even anger and aggression. Temperament can also lead to problems through influencing how children interpret their experiences. Whereas a fearful or easily frustrated child might be more likely to interpret a vague situation as a threat of some sort, another child might see the potential for a reward or positive experience in the same vague situation. For example, one child might approach a playground full of children and be fearful of being rejected or ignored, whereas another child might see the same situation as an opportunity to make a new friend. Over time, if a child falls into a pattern of interpreting vague or unfamiliar situations as potentially threatening, this can contribute to developing problems such as anxiety, depression, and aggression.

Remember the electric outlets? With my (Liliana's) daughter, I didn't need to make the outlets and plugs seem so threatening. Given that she was pretty reactive and fearful, a firm but gentle indication that the outlets were potentially dangerous was more than enough to teach her to stay away from the plugs, along with other dangerous things, like running into the street or wandering away from me and her father in public. But she was often anxious about other things, like birthday parties or dance class, and it took time and effort for her to learn that those situations were not as threatening and scary as she thought, so that she could approach them more comfortably. For my son, the plugs held tremendous allure for some reason, and over time we discovered that, for him, that tendency to approach things that were alluring would sometimes override any caution. It didn't matter how many times we worked on teaching him not to run into the street—if he saw something appealing across the street, like a playground or a toy, he ran toward it. We had different things to work on with him, like building his self-control, and we needed totally different strategies for teaching him to be safe.

CONCLUSION

It is important to remember that our children's social and emotional well-being or problems are not set in stone because of their temperament! A child's temperament characteristics are only one of many things that contribute to their chance of developing problems which are also determined by their experiences and contexts. This openness to experience gives parents, caregivers, and teachers the critical opportunity to support positive development with their children's temperament in mind. One focus of this book is to offer strategies for doing this. We can simultaneously validate who they are and shape their responses to be more adaptive, so that in the long run they are well adjusted.

The goal of this book is to provide parents with tools for effective parenting while keeping their children's temperament in mind. In the next two chapters, we describe specific temperament characteristics and the behaviors that are associated with them. In Chapter 3, we describe the biological systems that underlie children's temperament behaviors so that parents can have a better understanding of the roots of emotional and behavioral reactions. In Part II of the book, we dedicate a chapter to each of the characteristics that tend to present challenges for parents or that can increase children's chances of developing social, emotional, or behavioral problems. In those chapters we offer parents suggestions for supporting their children's positive development and well-being.

CHAPTER 2

TEMPERAMENT CHARACTERISTICS AND BEHAVIORS

The combination of emotional reactions and self-regulation leads to several temperament characteristics, or behavioral tendencies, in children, each with their own strengths, challenges, and adult responses that are more or less effective in supporting positive social–emotional outcomes. These temperament behavioral tendencies are continuous dimensions, with individuals falling along a normal range, from low to high and in between. These dimensions include fearfulness, fearlessness (including enjoying high intensity activities), frustration, impulsivity, inflexibility (including high fear and low effortful control), positive affect (happy, cheerful, or easygoing), and effortful control (including attention focus, self-control, and soothability). All children can be higher or lower in any of these dimensions, and the combination of characteristics can be thought of as a child's *temperament profile*.

All of these temperament characteristics map onto neurobiological systems that we discuss in Chapter 3. In Appendix A, we provide a tool for understanding your child's temperament profile based on these characteristics. In Part II of this book, we discuss each of the temperament characteristics, and sometimes the combination of characteristics, and how they tend to elicit different types of interactions and reactions from people and contexts. We focus on characteristics that can be challenging for parents and those that can lead to different trajectories of well-being for children in similar contexts. All the characteristics listed in the preceding paragraph contribute in some way to challenging behaviors, increasing risk or playing a protective role, and some we discuss jointly because of their combined impact.

Although temperament has its basis in biology, the behavioral characteristics and the development of the associated biological systems are open to social and environmental influences, meaning that contextual factors and social experiences can alter their expression and growth. It is important to note that children's temperament characteristics elicit different types of interactions and reactions from people and contexts, which can lead to varying outcomes for children in similar contexts, for example, siblings growing up in the same household. Another important point is that all temperament dimensions and profiles are normal, and everyone has a temperament profile marked by higher and lower levels of various traits. As we discuss these traits in more detail later in this chapter, we comment on their respective risk and protective capabilities given that some extremes can make social, emotional, or behavioral symptoms and problems more likely. The key temperament characteristics are summarized in Table 2.1.

FEARFULNESS

Fearfulness refers to high levels of fear, anxiety, or distress, often in situations that are new, unfamiliar, or vague. Fearful children might cry, whine, or throw temper tantrums when confronted with unfamiliar situations, tasks, and people, or they might withdraw or avoid these situations. Fearfulness can make children more careful and more likely to follow rules when they understand them to be for their safety or protection. They are also more likely to be compliant in school or other settings because they want to avoid the threat of getting in trouble.

TABLE 2.1. Temperament Characteristics and Behaviors Associated With Them

Dimension	Definition	Behaviors
Fearfulness	High fear, anxiety, or distress in response to novelty; sensitivity to cues of threat or the potential for negative consequences or punishment	• Inhibition, caution, withdrawal • Avoidance of novel, uncertain, or ambiguous situations
Fearlessness (and high-intensity pleasure)	Low fear, anxiety, or distress in response to novelty; little awareness of threat or the potential for negative consequences or punishment	• Lack of caution • Failure to see potential negative consequences • Enjoyment of high-intensity pleasure activities: risk taking and sensation seeking
Frustration	Frustration and anger when prevented from participating in rewarding experiences, approach is blocked, or when feeling confronted or attacked	• Quick or intense frustration or anger reactions • Argumentative, oppositional, or aggressive reactions
Impulsivity	Pursuit of potentially rewarding experiences without pause or consideration of potential negative consequences	• Quick reactions when faced with possible rewards • Difficulty waiting or pausing • Approach without caution • Failure to consider negative consequences before acting

(continues)

TABLE 2.1. Temperament Characteristics and Behaviors Associated With Them (*Continued*)

Dimension	Definition	Behaviors
Inflexibility (high fear and low effortful control)	Inability to accept a course of action that is unanticipated or different from the typical one; difficulty making choices when presented with options	• Distress when faced with a change in routine • Avoidance of unanticipated activities • Difficulty making new choices • Temper tantrums in response to a need for flexibility
Effortful control (including attention-focusing and inhibitory control)	An ability to focus and shift attention flexibly, inhibit automatic responses, and engage in a novel adaptive response rather than a well-practiced or automatic response that is not appropriate for the situation	• Ability to focus attention on relevant information • Ability to refrain from automatic responses • Measured responses in unanticipated situations • Flexible approach to changes in routine
Positive affect (cheerful and easygoing)	Propensity to experience and share joy and pleasure	• Appropriate smiling and laughter • Other expressions of enjoyment • Positive anticipation of activities expected to be enjoyable

TABLE 2.1. Temperament Characteristics and Behaviors Associated With Them (*Continued*)

Dimension	Definition	Behaviors
Soothability	Ability to regulate emotions and to use caregivers to lower arousal	• Quick recovery from distress • Positive responses to parental efforts to soothe

However, expressions of fear are not always the norm for these children because a number of them are so good at avoiding, and getting their parents to accommodate this avoidance, that there is never a cause for a lot of distress. For example, a fearful child who is able to refuse to participate in activities that are not familiar or comfortable, such as trying out a new sport or hobby, or a child who can always get out of going to a birthday party where she might encounter unfamiliar peers, is not likely to show a lot of fearful distress. Of course, all children respond with fear to certain experiences, such as a painful medical procedure, and there are developmentally appropriate fears, such as when preschoolers are afraid of the dark. Research has shown that the hallmark of a fearful child is a higher level of fear or anxiety in situations that other children tend to find less upsetting or neutral. We think of children who are only reactive in this manner to social situations as shy, yet shyness involves the same neurobiological foundations.

FEARLESSNESS

Fearlessness represents the other end of the fear temperament dimension. Children described as fearless are so low in fear reactivity that they do not slow down in dangerous situations. The scientific thinking is that fearless children have limited sensitivity to cues of threat, danger, punishment, or nonreward, which means that their attention to such details is not effective. This information does not get treated with priority, as it does in individuals with some level of fearful reactivity. Moreover, engagement of the fear-related neurobehavioral system in terms of the brain and peripheral activity results in a slowing down or stopping of motor responses (i.e., freezing), which does not occur for fearless individuals. These are the kids who are likely to take chances, running into the street despite prohibitions, jumping off cliffs or bridges into the water, and going really fast on bicycles and skateboards. They are more likely to experience enjoyment or pleasure from high-intensity or risky activities, finding these rewarding.

An underactive fear response can be problematic, resulting in unintended injuries and challenging parents in terms of setting appropriate limits. This is especially true if children are also lower in effortful control, described shortly. If the child is not tuned in to potential threats in the environment, they will struggle to keep in mind a consequence parents or teachers have articulated for undesirable behaviors. In other words, telling a fearless child the consequence for misbehaving might not have much of an effect if their mind is focused on a really fun thing they want to do. In the long term, a fearless temperament style has been shown to put some children at risk for acting-out difficulties, including noncompliance and aggression, which often turn into academic difficulties and can sometimes lead to delinquency and substance use issues.

FRUSTRATION

Easily frustrated children have a difficult time with limits being placed on them and their goals being blocked. Experimental studies have shown that these approach-oriented individuals quickly become frustrated when they are not able to obtain the desired reward (e.g.,

Gatze-Kopp et al., 2015). Frustration can also result from other people doing things "wrong," that is, not in a manner the child had envisioned or preferred. Often, parents catch on to this temperament style and are accommodating so as to keep the peace in the household. However, this can lead to more problems as children find that their angry reactions can get them what they want or get them out of doing things they don't want to do. In addition, peers are typically not as savvy as adults when it comes to preventing frustration from leading to conflict. Thus, easily frustrated children often complain about their friends not playing games or following rules "right," or taking toys that they want, and experience less satisfying peer relationships more broadly. Because the frustrated child often reacts with anger, they tend to draw anger from others—parents, teachers, and peers—and this can lead to a detrimental cycle that in some children increases the chances of oppositional, aggressive behavior problems.

IMPULSIVITY

Impulsive children tend to do first and think second and are strongly motivated to go after the things that they want or that they experience as rewarding. They often struggle in situations that demand persistence and can appear to avoid putting effort into things, appearing lazy. However, it is not that they do not want to put forth the effort per se. They just want to see a payoff for their effort right away, not at some point down the road. This reward-focused behavior can be coupled with a moderate or high level of fearfulness, so that a child goes after low-risk rewards (e.g., wanting dessert or wanting to play their video game), but it can also be coupled with fearlessness or high-intensity pleasure, so that the approach behaviors and sensation seeking don't have an easily accessible brake. This creates a double jeopardy for them: an enhanced reward approach with little or no braking system.

In general, what underlies impulsivity, both the fear-modulated and fearless types, is typically a less advanced ability to regulate emotions and put brakes on behavior. Impulsive children process information differently from their fearless counterparts—it is not necessarily that they lack sensitivity to cues of danger and nonreward. Instead, they are less able to inhibit or stop themselves from making suboptimal choices or behaviors, and they struggle with conflict resolution (i.e., selecting the most optimal response when choices are available). In fact, a hallmark of an impulsive child involves a limited *behavioral inhibition capacity*, defined as the ability to inhibit or stop a previously favored response that is now inappropriate for a particular situation or context and engaging in an adaptive but less favored response instead. As toddlers, impulsive children grab for candy bars and gum in the grocery store check-out lines as their mothers can be heard voicing prohibitions. Similar to the fearless children, impulsive children often find themselves in dangerous situations: in the street going after the ball, skateboarding home after dark, riding a bicycle or a scooter without a helmet.

For some impulsive children who are not fearless, their impulsivity might present as forgetting to raise their hand in class before blurting out an answer, or grabbing for dessert on the counter even when they know they are not to have dessert until after dinner. Whether the situation is dangerous or mundane, impulsive children are characteristically not able to stop, wait, think, and assess the best way to approach a situation. Not only is impulsivity a risk factor when it comes to attention-deficit/hyperactivity disorder, it is actually a symptom cluster in its extreme form, that is, when impulsive acts cause distress or impairment and occur in the context of inattention and hyperactivity. Impulsive children are also at risk for other problems, with elevated chances of struggling with conduct problems and substance use as teens, given a lack of appropriate support from their caregivers, schools, and communities.

In understanding how best to support your child who tends to do impulsive things, it is useful to understand the source of that impulsivity. Some children might be highly reward oriented (reward/approach), so they go after things that give them joy and pleasure without stopping to plan for the most effective way to attain it (which requires effortful control). Other children might dive into high-intensity activities because that is rewarding to them (high-intensity pleasure), and if that is coupled with low fear, they might do these things in ways that are unsafe. However, for children higher in effortful control, it is also possible to experience pleasure or joy from high-intensity activities, although usually in a more careful way, such as following a plan (e.g., making sure appropriate equipment is available and properly functioning).

INFLEXIBILITY

Inflexibility can lead children to struggle with adaptation to any change in the routine or deviation from their expectations and predictable activities. They come to be inflexible through different neurobiological pathways, with their rigidity typically stemming from frequently avoiding change to mitigate anxiety or discomfort, most likely coupled with limited brain-based attentional, emotional, or behavioral regulatory capacity, as we discuss in Chapter 3. In other words, fearfulness, together with low effortful control, described in the next section, can lead to inflexibility. The very extreme form of rigidity to alleviate fear and anxiety can turn into obsessive-compulsive disorder, wherein rituals are performed to manage anxiety or prevent it from occurring.

Short of engaging in full-blown compulsive routines to mitigate obsessions and related fear or anxiety, some highly fearful children adapt a rigid temperament style in an effort to achieve the same goal: "If I make sure things stay exactly the same and everything in my life is completely predictable, I don't have to experience those unpleasant and uncomfortable feelings." Of course, this is not a conscious or voluntary decision. Instead, this temperament style becomes dominant simply because of largely unconscious emotional and learning processes at work. Children understand that they do not like feeling fear and learn that maintaining a rigid behavioral stance ensures they do not have to be afraid, at least, a lot of the time. Avoiding negative emotions is rapidly learned, meaning that whatever allowed the individual to avoid a bad feeling is instantly more readily deployed as a strategy going forward. When this is repeated over time, this temperament style becomes ingrained. However, the second pathway that leads to inflexible behaviors is also powerful, as children who struggle to resolve a conflict between different available choices would rather avoid having to make a choice, which they do not have to do when everything in their daily life happens in exactly the same manner.

To better understand the sources of a child's inflexible behaviors, it is useful for parents to understand the degree to which fearfulness and low effortful control might be contributing. At the extreme, this type of inflexibility may become the basis for a diagnosis of an autism spectrum disorder, along with communication and language problems. Regardless of the pathway, the end result is the same in terms of the emotions and behaviors parents have to address: Inflexible children experience distress and can have significant tantrums and meltdowns when something that they did not anticipate takes place (e.g., field trip instead of a regular class schedule, going on vacation or being away from home, a substitute teacher who wants to do things differently).

EFFORTFUL CONTROL

Children higher in self-regulation are less demanding and challenging to parents because of their ability to modulate their emotions and behaviors. Temperament researchers refer to this self-regulation as *effortful control* to convey children's ability to apply effort to focus their attention on what is important, shift their attention away from distractions, persist in an activity that is demanding, and even initiate an activity that they don't really want to do. Both the ability to regulate attention and the ability to inhibit automatic thoughts and behaviors contribute to children's effortful control. A child can be higher in one or the other, or both, to demonstrate good effortful control. Children who are higher in effortful control tend to evoke more positive interactions with their parents and other adults, they are more self-directed, and parents can be less intrusive or controlling in their efforts to manage behavioral challenges. In fact, these children tend to display fewer behavioral challenges in general.

Children with more efficient emotion regulation systems facilitated by physiological processes linking brain and behavior (discussed in the next chapter) are less likely to have very intense emotional reactions, or they are more likely to recover more quickly from an emotional reaction. Parents experience these children as easily soothable, and, in fact, these children are pretty good at soothing themselves when they are upset.

We should note that *reactivity* (i.e., approach and avoidance tendencies) comes earlier in development, in infancy, setting the stage for the later development of effortful control. Effortful control, which develops later, relies on executive functions, or on soothability, which is related to respiratory sinus arrhythmia (discussed in the next chapter), which primarily happens in the toddler and preschool years. Self-regulated children are more likely to start out as balanced in terms of their approach and avoidance processes, facilitating the emergence of flexible and voluntarily controlled attention, which provides the basis for effective self-regulation. Advanced self-regulation abilities are protective with respect to numerous important outcomes, reducing the risk for most frequent childhood symptoms or disorders (e.g., anxiety, depression, behavior problems) and enhancing the likelihood of peer acceptance and academic achievement.

POSITIVE AFFECT

Cheerful or easygoing children—that is, children higher in positive affect or emotions—are just that: happy to do what they are doing, happy to shift gears and do something else, enjoying interactions with family and friends. In some ways, parents of these children have won the temperament lottery. As infants, they smile a lot, do not make a big fuss about being put down for a nap in a new place, handle the introduction of new foods easily, and adapt to day care. When they become toddlers, they enjoy interacting with other children and go to day care and birthday parties without challenging their parents to elevate their behavior management techniques. Cheerful, easygoing children are curious preschoolers who are eager to try new things and experience different social situations. They are typically well liked by their teachers and peers and enjoy supportive relationships. Is there anything that can go wrong for these children? Research suggests that their developmental trajectories are bright (e.g., Lengua & Wachs, 2012). However, there is one potential downside to being cheerful or easygoing: These children may not develop resilience-related skills because their temperament style does not elicit contextual reactions that make such skills essential for adaptation and success.

We do not include in this book individual chapters on effortful control or cheerful characteristics because children exhibiting high levels of these do not typically present parents with challenging responses that require reflection and guidance. Children who are easygoing or well-regulated are generally able to successfully manage their behavior at home, in school, and with peers. They can follow instructions, wait their turn, and manage their fear or frustration so it doesn't get the better of them. A child might have good self-regulation skills and also be fearful or easily frustrated, or high in reward or approach motivation. However, their self-regulation might modulate these emotional and behavioral reactions so that they tend to be more adaptive, matching the demands of a particular situation. Children who are low in self-regulation tend to have more challenging behaviors when they are also fearful, high in frustration or reward orientation. We address these challenging behaviors in the next chapters.

On the other end of the cheerful or positive affect dimension is low positive affect. *Low positive affect* is just that: a limited propensity to experience joy and pleasure from various activities. In addition to a potential long-term risk for depression, a disorder for which an inability to enjoy inherently pleasurable activities is a symptom (i.e., anhedonia), children who are low in positive affect can pose challenges to their parents for a couple of reasons. One is that it might be hard to find something that motivates, interests, or excites these children. It might be difficult to entice them to join a fun family activity or to find a reward that consistently motivates them to do their chores or practice their musical instrument.

Another challenge posed by children who are low in positive affect is that parents need positive reinforcement from their children. In other words, we rely on positive reactions from our children, their smiles and laughter, to have a sense of being a competent parent; doing the right thing as a parent; providing our children with appropriate, stimulating, or entertaining activities. In the absence of such reactions, or when these positive responses are muted or rare, it is difficult to maintain the self-perception that one is on track as a parent or being assured that one is making the best choices for their children.

We don't include in this book a separate chapter on children with low positive affect because there is not much research on what type of parenting is effective with these children. We know that children who are high in positive affect tend to elicit more warmth and engagement from their parents, so we can infer the opposite is true for children with low positive affect. To counter that, parents can build a stronger positive relationship through engaging in Child-Led Time, described in full in Chapter 10. Research addressing depression has shown that behavioral activation can work to increase joy and positive affect (e.g., Dimidjian et al., 2008). *Behavioral activation* refers to using one's behaviors or activities to increase positive or pleasant emotions. Usually, we do things because we enjoy them. The idea of behavioral activation is to grow to enjoy things because we do them. By engaging in a particular activity, the person doesn't have to feel motivated to do it to still gain some benefit from doing it. Exercise is a good example. We also encourage our principle of adding "icing on the cake, and putting a cherry on top." By this we mean that you can increase the reward value of important events, such as family gatherings, outings, or time with friends, by working together with your child to plan to incorporate activities and experiences that the child finds enjoyable.

Another way to increase the positive value of experiences is to incorporate gratitude practice. This is the simple practice of slowing down to notice, reflect on, and savor the positive or rewarding aspects of an event, experience, or day. These experiences can be big or small, and if it's hard to find something positive or rewarding about an event, we can notice and acknowledge a small part of it. Although it is important not to force expressions of gratitude or to encourage false statements, because this can build resentment, everyone in the family is likely to benefit from more attention to positives by stopping to "smell the roses."

OTHER TEMPERAMENT CHARACTERISTICS

There are several characteristics with notable individual differences that are considered to be temperament but do not typically pose challenges for parents or increase children's risk for developing social, emotional, or behavioral problems. These include activity level, shyness, and affiliativeness. *Activity level* can be observed as early as infancy, and for some children it may stand out as a defining characteristic—someone who is always on the go or has busy hands. Activity may pose risk in the context of certain additional attributes, such as deficient behavior or emotion regulation and impulsivity, which could potentially develop into symptoms of attention-deficit/hyperactivity disorder. However, in concert with other traits, a high activity level can be related to positive adjustment and social competence, such as when a well-regulated child is able to get going easily and be ready to start their day, or excel in sports or exploration of the outdoors.

Shyness is generally not a recipe for adjustment problems, because children who are slow to warm up in new situations or around new people are typically able to develop supportive and meaningful relationships with others and are comfortable with familiar adults and peers. However, in the context of rigidity or poor regulation, being slow to warm up can turn into temper tantrums when the child is presented with new social situations, making it difficult to warm up at all and creating challenges for caregivers who often feel pressured to accommodate this wariness of new people. These challenges are discussed in Chapters 5 and 8.

Affiliativeness is an interesting trait that can be observed as early as the first year of life, when it is manifested as cuddliness. Not the same as extraversion or sociability, affiliativeness has to do with desiring closeness with others, initially in tangible terms, seeking out opportunities for physical proximity, and later on a relational level, being comforted by intimate relationships with others and opting for fewer close connections as opposed to many superficial ones. Although generally positive and promoting of well-being, individuals high in affiliativeness may be less resilient if opportunities for such close relationships are not afforded by their circumstances, such as when multiple moves are required because of the parents' jobs. Once again, we do not discuss this further because, in general, affiliativeness does not present challenges for parents or an increased risk for problems.

CONCLUSION

Most children's temperament profiles are marked not by a dominance of one temperament characteristic but, more often, by a mixture of characteristics and tandem actions of underlying neurobiological mechanisms, as we describe in the next chapter. The traits we have noted in this chapter also gain their importance from context, whereby, depending on the rest of the temperament profile, as well as environmental circumstances, they may pose a risk for, or provide protection from, developing problems. It is important to note that when we speak about risk or protection with respect to social, emotional, or behavioral problems or symptoms, these are *probabilistic*, meaning that the odds of developing significant problems are either increased or diminished by particular characteristics. These trajectories are not guaranteed, in part because they also depend on a variety of contextual factors, on the micro (relationships with parents, caregivers, nuclear family) and macro (societal, community, school) levels. In early childhood, context is largely determined by family, parenting, and the parent–child relationship, and so it can be readily altered in a healthier direction. For example, parents of a fearful child can become less accommodating in their approach. For this reason, in this book we focus on parenting and the parent–child relationship while also recognizing that other contexts play a critical role in children's development. As such, other adults in a child's life, including teachers, coaches, physicians, and mental health care providers, can also benefit children by incorporating an understanding of temperament into their work and interactions with children and families.

In Appendix A, we include a tool that allows you to reflect on and understand your child's temperament. Although you might already have thoughts about which characteristics are lower or higher for your child, this tool can provide a perspective on where your child falls on each dimension and give you a better idea of their temperament profile.

CHAPTER 3

BRAIN AND BODY SYSTEMS UNDERLYING TEMPERAMENT

You often hear people say things like "Their brain is wired differently," or "they were born that way." This chapter is meant to shed light on how temperament has its roots in biology and how that biology shapes how we engage with the world. We hope this chapter provides a better understanding of where your child's emotional reactivity and regulation behaviors come from. For some, this might seem like information that is more technical than you want; however, we encourage you to power through, because this foundational information is in fact relevant to parenting efforts and can help guide them. Learning about the biological underpinnings of temperament can help clarify your expectations regarding your child's behavior, providing a better understanding of responses that are more easily attainable for your child as well as of the amount and type of support they may need in a particular situation. Every temperament characteristic provides strengths as well as challenges in certain situations.

If you ever took a biology class in school, you might remember learning about the *fight–flight* response system. Temperament stems largely from approach (fight), inhibition (flight), and freeze systems that are rooted in the sympathetic branch of the autonomic nervous system, as well as the parasympathetic and prefrontal cortex (frontal lobe) brain systems that help children regulate their emotions. In this chapter, we describe these systems and their functions. They represent coordination between different areas of the brain, as well as peripheral activity (i.e., in biological systems outside of the brain), as a foundation for motivation, emotion, and behavior. Although identifying some aspects of these systems and the mechanisms behind their coordination remains a work in progress, a great deal has already been learned and is summarized in this chapter.

TEMPERAMENT FOUNDATIONS IN THE BRAIN

When we say that temperament is biologically based, we mean that the foundations for what we have come to understand as temperament rest largely in the brain. It is one thing to recognize the brain as the basis for behavior, and specifically temperament, but another to identify brain activity and development contributions to emotional reactivity and regulation, which we turn to next.

Measuring Brain Activity: Functional Magnetic Resonance Imaging and Electroencephalography

The current knowledge base comes from research that has made connections between central nervous system activity, often measured via functional magnetic resonance imaging (fMRI) or electroencephalography (EEG) technology, and observed behavior. In brief, fMRI techniques rely on measuring changes in blood flow, and blood oxygenation in particular. In fMRI imaging studies a research participant is asked to engage in a task that is thought to activate a particular part of the brain, and fluctuations in blood flow are observed. These tasks can require language, numerical, or emotional processing. Fluctuations, visualized through this approach, can be interpreted as changes in brain activity, or the coordinated action of different networks, depending on the nature of the task being performed. One critical takeaway is that, even with this sophisticated brain imaging technology, the interpretation of observed effects (i.e., changes in blood oxygenation, which are viewed as a marker of brain activity) is entirely dependent on behaviors required by the task the participant engages in during an experiment. Observed effects cannot be explained in a meaningful way without appreciating the participant's response to the task. This required response or behavior is interpreted very broadly and sometimes involves attention to pictures or other digital visual content being presented in the scanner and other times entails simply resting. Nonetheless, knowing exactly what the participant is doing when the snapshot of brain activity is produced is essential to being able to make sense of fMRI findings.

EEG is an older technology that is still in wide use today because of a number of important advantages. For example, although fMRI is superior for determining *localization* of brain activity, EEG provides a better picture related to the *timing* of brain activity relative to what the participant is doing in the experimental task.

Animal studies, which afford greater experimental control and more direct access to physiology, have proved important in enhancing our understanding of brain–behavior connections relevant to approach and avoidance systems. For example, the pioneering work addressing reward- and punishment-oriented systems we describe later in this chapter was conducted with animals, supporting the conclusion that these systems are in fact separate, with individual differences in sensitivity for each.

Behavioral Inhibition and Activation

As mentioned earlier, we all have a fight–flight biological system that helps us respond to the experiences and environments we encounter. How we respond can be affected by the balance of our fight and flight tendencies. One framework for understanding the biological roots of this involves the behavioral inhibition and activation systems (Gray, 1994). The motivation to respond to a situation by withdrawing is thought to be part of an avoidance system, which has acquired a number of different names in the scientific literature, including *behavioral inhibition system* (BIS), *fight–flight system* (sometimes referred to as the *fight–flight–freeze system*), and *threat avoidance system*. Regardless of the specific term used, what they all have in common is a focus on responses to signals of danger, punishment, and nonreward (i.e., not getting the desired outcome), that is, something bad potentially happening. This responsiveness includes readiness for action (arousal level) and heightened attention to cues of threat or danger.

Behavioral inhibition is a tendency to withdraw or react negatively in response to novelty or uncertainty, including people, places, events, and objects. Some children tend to avoid novel or uncertain situations because they fear the unknown potential for something bad to happen. Behavioral inhibition is typically expressed as hesitation to approach novel or unclear situations, and it is experienced together with fear at the emotional level. However, effective avoidance can also *prevent* a fear response, which is very reinforcing. For example, when someone avoids a feared situation and successfully prevents feeling afraid (eliminating the uncomfortable or negative feeling), they are much more likely to use the same avoidance strategy in the future. This occurs because the dreaded fear was avoided, which is the desired outcome, and so it is more likely the action that preceded it will be taken again. The BIS (Gray, 1994) is thought to support fear and avoidance, is oriented to punishment, and is capable of hindering behavior that serves to achieve approach- or reward-related goals.

Biological models of sensitivity to reward and approach invoke the *behavioral activation system* (BAS; Gray, 1994) in their explanations and definitions. The BAS is a counterpart to the BIS. This system focuses an individual on potential rewards, heightens the urge to experience or obtain the rewards, and motivates approach toward and efforts to obtain them. Connections with the fight–flight reaction system that is responsible for preparing to stand one's ground or fight for what one wants are made because confronting an opponent involves approach and typically serves to remove barriers that are blocking a desired reward or goal. As such, this system has a complicated set of emotional implications, including anticipation of reward and positive outcomes, delight and enjoyment in obtaining rewards, and anger or frustration when rewards are blocked, potentially resulting in aggression.

Left Versus Right Dominance in the Frontal Cortex

Well-established models describing neurobiological foundations of the BAS and the fight side of the fight–flight reaction system, as well as the BIS and flight (and/or freeze) aspect focus on patterns of brain activity in the frontal portion of the cortex, the part of the brain right behind the forehead. The pattern of interest is the asymmetrical activation of the frontal cortex, or a lateralization of approach avoidance activity. This refers to more or less activity in the left versus right side of the frontal lobe. According to a sizable body of work, the left and right frontal cortical regions are asymmetrically related to approach and avoidance motivational and emotional tendencies. Traits reflecting an enduring approach orientation and prioritization of rewards (as opposed to punishment) are indicated by relatively stronger left frontal activation, and a greater tendency toward inhibition and withdrawal is indicated by dominant right frontal activation. This lateralization is typically measured with EEG recordings and, more recently, with functional near-infrared spectroscopy (fNIRS), which is similar to fMRI insofar as brain regions receiving an increased ratio of oxygenated blood are presumed to be activated; oxygenation is again used as a proxy for brain activity.

Most of us have heard of "left brain" and "right brain" people, referring to whether someone is more oriented to logic, analytic thinking, and language, versus more creative and intuitive, respectively. When we talk about lateralization of motivation and emotions, many people are often surprised to hear that the specialization of the two hemispheres goes beyond language and creativity. How do we understand this differential contribution of the right and left frontal cortical areas? In terms of the underlying neurophysiology, both subcortical (i.e., the limbic system) and cortical regions are involved in processing emotions and generating responses. The limbic system is the part of the brain involved in the primary responses needed for survival, such as instincts and basic emotions. Activation of the BIS involves the amygdala, basal ganglia, and hypothalamus, all parts of the limbic system, as well as the right dorsolateral prefrontal cortex and the right temporal region. These parts of the brain are often associated with attention control and problem solving. Activity in these areas accounts for a pattern of right-hemisphere–dominant frontal EEG activity. The BAS, on the other hand, involves the corticolimbic–striatal–thalamic network, the area of the brain associated with movement and reward. The BAS also relies on dopamine pathways leading from the ventral tegmental area, which is associated with reward processing, to the subcortical and frontal cortical regions, which favor left frontal activation. Taken together, dopamine pathways serve a variety of critical functions, such as movement and neuroendocrine control, as well as reward motivation and executive functions, which we describe shortly. Although EEG asymmetry measures electrical activity at the cortex of the frontal lobe, the pattern of lateralization (i.e., right vs. left frontal dominance) reflects underlying brain activity that involves limbic structures critical to emotional processes (e.g., the amygdala).

Approach and avoidance processes and the frontal brain activation asymmetry thought to underlie their tandem action are important to several temperament dimensions discussed in this book. Fearfulness stems from an overactive BIS system that predisposes children to see and avoid cues of threat in their environment. Intensive developmental studies conducted by Nathan Fox and colleagues (Degnan et al., 2008) have shown that infants who are reactive to novelty become toddlers who tend to hesitate to approach unfamiliar objects and people and later turn into socially reticent preschoolers. For example, during the preschool period children who started out as right frontal dominant in terms of their brain activity avoid interacting with unfamiliar peers, even in a situation where multiple children are present, no one knows each other beforehand, and there are lots of fun games and toys available. While other children engage with their new peers, these socially reticent children are involved in solo play, carefully watching others at the same time. It is not surprising that, under some circumstances, this tendency portends later anxiety disorders, social anxiety in particular, although not for everyone.

Fearlessness represents the other extreme of this temperament spectrum and maps onto left frontal dominance in terms of neurobiology. The inability of right frontal regions to provide meaningful input is thought to be responsible for the bias or tendency to favor rewards and dismiss threats displayed by fearless children. Frequent or intense frustration is also associated with relative left frontal activation, which supports approach tendencies and a reward-seeking focus. Expression of this temperament trait typically occurs when potential rewards are blocked, so approach motives cannot be readily satisfied. Although positive emotions often accompany approach and related actions, frustration can also arise in children who have relatively greater left frontal activation, which can be manifested as crying, whining, screaming, and disruptive behaviors.

Coordination Across the Hemispheres

Now that we have reviewed the foundation of approach and avoidance tendencies, we should talk about regulation. First, because the emphasis so far has been on lateralization of emotion and motivation, it is important to note the BIS and BAS are thought to work in tandem, in large part because of the coordinated action across the two hemispheres, as depicted in Figure 3.1.

It is important to note that everyone's nervous system supports BAS and BIS activation, which can respond differently in different

FIGURE 3.1. Coordination of Behavioral Activation System and Behavioral Inhibition System Across the Two Brain Hemispheres

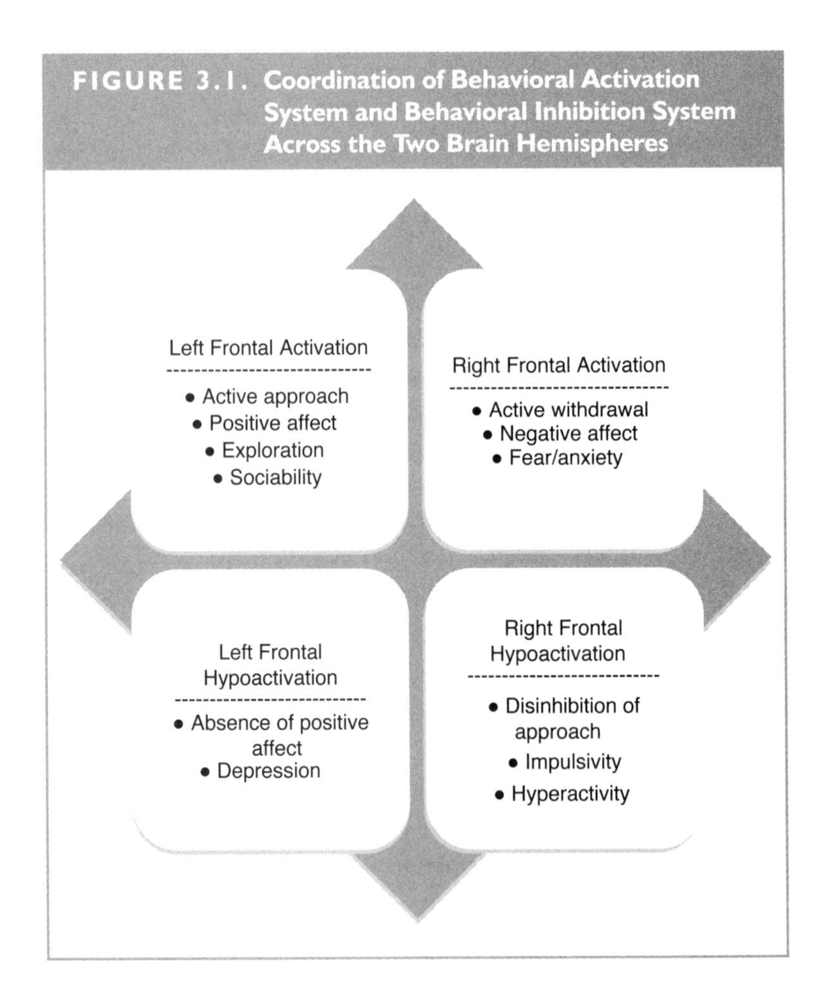

situations. We observe approach tendencies when activation of the BAS is stronger than activation of the BIS, and we observe avoidance tendencies when activation of the BIS is stronger than that of the BAS. So, it is the balance of these systems, sensitive to situational demands, that motivates behavior and drives temperament characteristics.

Having greater left frontal activation relative to right frontal activation is associated with positive emotions. In children with too little left frontal activation, we expect to see low positive mood, or dysphoria. Diminished positive emotions, in turn, increase the risk for depression. This may not seem surprising given the fact that depression is characterized not only by sadness and irritability but also by anhedonia—that is, the inability to enjoy inherently pleasurable activities. Too much right frontal activity is associated with fear, anxiety, and avoidance. Not enough right frontal activation (i.e., hypoactivity) might show up as fearlessness. Too much left frontal dominance might underlie impulsive and hyperactive behaviors. As you can see, balance in left and right lateral frontal activation is adaptive.

A person who tends to be more BIS motivated will, in general, show more fearfulness or caution in situations they perceive as threatening a negative outcome. A person who is more BAS motivated will be more oriented toward seeing and pursuing the potential reward in a situation and might be more likely to approach. Neurodevelopmental science typically considers approach and avoidance as traits (i.e., long-standing and stable attributes). Related systems regulate each other in the moment, with their effects easily observable in behavior. Have you ever noticed how, when your generally outgoing child is all of a sudden quiet and not talkative at times, she might be especially worried about something? I (Masha) have seen this a few times with my daughter on the way to the orthodontist's office for a longer appointment, presumably because of anticipation that something more complicated, uncomfortable, and possibly painful could take place. This is BIS and right frontal activation dominating the BAS and the left hemisphere counterpart, which can happen even when someone is typically more BAS dominant. In a recent article, Gartstein et al. (2019) showed that how EEG asymmetry changes across childhood are a function of the left and right frontal activation balancing act, with each exerting some influence over growth in the other.

The regulatory effects between the BIS and BAS are notable as early as the first year of life. More flexible self-regulation that allows for dynamic adaptations, voluntary action, and an ability to discern most effective courses of action emerges starting in the second year of life. Although not always apparent on the behavioral level during the "terrible 2s," this attention-based regulatory capacity is starting to emerge, and continues to develop into young adulthood, as frontal lobe structures mature. Attentional systems supporting this emerging self-regulation, including the lateral prefrontal cortex (PFC) and anterior cingulate cortex (ACC), undergo rapid development in infancy and early childhood. These areas support *executive functions*, which include the ability to focus attention on relevant elements; shift attention away from irrelevant ones; and inhibit thoughts, emotions, or behaviors that are suboptimal responses in a particular situation. Executive functions represent a key ability for managing thoughts, emotions, and behaviors. In early childhood, the physical maturation of brain structures and changes in connections among brain networks provide the foundation for advanced self-regulation, allowing children to prioritize sensory information, resolve conflict, and select between alternative responses (e.g., determining which would be best under the current circumstance). This regulation is considered "top-down" control and is essential for school readiness and academic success, allowing children to regulate their emotions and behaviors, pay attention, and learn. Executive functions provide top-down regulation of approach and avoidance cues, modulating emotions (both processing and expression) and inhibiting impulses in motivationally or emotionally significant situations (e.g., evaluating a threat or reward). High levels of impulsivity, anxiety, and depression can result from ineffective top-down control over approach and avoidance processes. In the context of impulsivity, for example, limited executive functions supported primarily by the frontal lobe structures (but also by the anterior cingulate, which is typically considered part of the subcortical limbic system) do not effectively prevent inappropriate or potentially dangerous behavior.

Consistently high levels of approach and avoidance behavioral tendencies are also viewed as extreme temperament, thought to reflect deficient top-down regulation, or executive function response, to approach and avoidance reactions. My (Masha's) team is currently conducting research, funded by the National Science Foundation, aimed at discerning these complicated connections by considering changes in the underlying neurophysiology (frontal EEG asymmetry).

TEMPERAMENT FOUNDATIONS IN THE BODY

The body is also involved in providing a biological basis for temperament, facilitating different behavioral patterns through individual differences in physiology. Whereas peripheral processes, such as heart rate and hormones that circulate in our blood, are driven by brain activity, which can stimulate initiation and maintain the response, there is also considerable feedback from bodily reactions that inform brain activity in turn.

Heart Rate Variability: Respiratory Sinus Arrhythmia

Respiratory sinus arrhythmia (RSA), derived from an electrocardiogram (ECG), is widely used to measure parasympathetic activation, related to emotional reactivity and regulation in childhood. RSA refers to the variability in our heart rate related to breathing. When we breathe in, our heart rate quickens a bit, and when we breathe out it slows down a little. This variability in heart rate in response to respiration is primarily linked to activity of the vagus nerve. Vagal influence diminishes during inhalation, resulting in heart rate acceleration, and increases during exhalation, causing heart rate deceleration. This characteristic respiratory rhythm of RSA provides a noninvasive measure of cardiac vagal tone and peripheral regulation. Both traitlike RSA and changes in RSA are related to temperament. In infants, higher overall RSA occurs with lower negative emotionality and less calming needed from parents. In older children, high RSA is related to better social skills, more efficient mental processes, and better behavioral and emotion regulation. In infancy, a higher RSA often translates into being more easily soothed, and children with a higher RSA are better at calming down or soothing themselves when upset. In general, RSA underlies an ability to lower one's level of arousal.

Changes in cardiac vagal tone in response to challenges reflect the vagal brake through which rapid inhibition and disinhibition of vagal tone to the heart (i.e., via the sinoatrial node, which is the heart's pacemaker) can rapidly mobilize or calm an individual. These changes can be studied in the laboratory by measuring RSA before and after presenting a mild stressor, such as having the parent briefly withdraw from communicating. Decreases in RSA (or inhibition of the vagal tone) have been shown to be adaptive in research participants when faced with laboratory challenges, especially when followed by recovery. Infant research has shown the importance of the vagal brake in the regulation of attention and social behaviors that require an awareness of the environment and the ability to engage or disengage. In sum, traitlike RSA reflects reactive tendencies, whereas decreases in RSA during challenging encounters are markers of attention-based regulation of emotion and behavior. Children described as cheerful and easygoing benefit from more optimal RSA, or vagal tone, as well as more advanced executive functions supported by frontal lobe maturation, with both facilitating better emotion regulation.

The Stress Hormone: Cortisol

Activity of the stress-sensitive hypothalamic–pituitary–adrenocortical (HPA) system has been examined in temperament research as well, with the primary focus on its role in modulating the effects of exposure to stress (see Figure 3.2). Activation of the HPA system results in the release of cortisol from the adrenal glands into the bloodstream, and minimally invasive procedures allow for its measurement through saliva, fingernail, and hair samples, making cortisol the most frequently studied component of the stress response system. In terms of links to temperament, higher approach tendencies and less advanced regulation co-occur with elevated cortisol levels in preschool-age children. Higher morning cortisol in preschool children has also been noted in those experiencing fewer positive emotions and in children whose mothers report a history of depression. Laboratory-induced stressors are used most widely to study cortisol levels of older children and adults.

Studies including young children have often addressed changes in the diurnal cortisol rhythm in response to stressors encountered in everyday life, for example, the beginning of the school day. The HPA system displays a daily rhythm: Higher levels of cortisol typically occur in the morning, and decrease by bedtime, often to near zero. This typical daily pattern can be leveraged to make interpretations about children's temperament and stress responses. Cortisol changes related to tasks administered in an experiment have also been observed; for example, in one study (Eisenberg et al., 2009), increased concentrations of cortisol were noted in a preschool sample when considering levels before and after a frustration-eliciting experimental task.

FIGURE 3.2. The Hypothalamic–Pituitary–Adrenocortical System Responding to Stress, Releasing Cortisol From the Adrenal Glands Into the Bloodstream

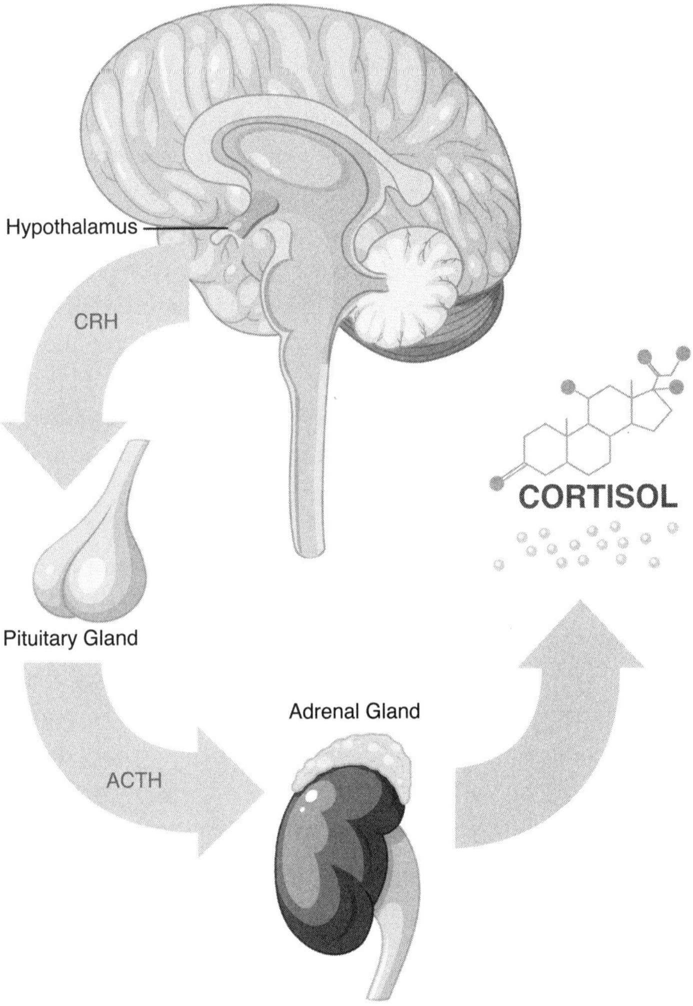

Note. CRH = corticotropin-releasing hormone; ACTH = adrenocorticotropic hormone. Image by brgfx on Freepik.

It is important to note that consistently high levels of cortisol are thought to have detrimental effects on the functioning of the HPA system by damaging the regulatory mechanism, which appears to lose sensitivity required for effective control, no longer increasing and decreasing concentrations according to the environmental circumstances. In fact, long-term exposure to adversity seems to result in *hypocortisolism*, or consistently low levels of cortisol, attributed to this HPA dysregulation. We should also note that the relationship between HPA reactivity or cortisol concentrations and top-down control afforded by executive functions may be bidirectional given that high cortisol concentrations appear to disrupt the development of executive control and deficient executive functions are related to excessive HPA reactivity. This disruption of executive function development may be one important mechanism behind the contribution of environmental adversity to poor self-regulation.

Coordination Among Emotion- and Self-Regulation Systems

The multiple systems we have discussed contribute to emotion regulation, with infants' and children's reactivity, executive or effortful control, RSA, and the HPA system all working together. To understand how children manage their emotions and what we can do to support their self-regulation, we need to understand how these systems might each be contributing or working together, and this might vary for different children. Much of what we have learned about how these systems work together comes from research conducted with infants. It may be surprising to learn about the considerable amount of research focused on self-regulation in infancy. Although babies are not very good at regulating themselves, studying their efforts sheds light on where regulation comes from, informing our understanding of development and efforts to promote regulatory skills. Infant physiological regulatory capacity is often studied via laboratory procedures, most commonly in the *Still-Face Procedure* (SFP), which has become the hallmark of emotion regulation assessment in infancy. The SFP was designed to capture infants' active contributions to social interactions. It aims to elicit infant distress, mild to moderate in intensity, in response to caregiver's display of a "still face" (i.e., emotionless, flat facial expression) and absence of any vocal communication, providing a window to subsequent regulation efforts. The still-face expression is typically followed by caregiver's return to play with the child (reunion) and can be repeated to obtain an additional measure of infant's self-regulation in response to a caregiver's emotional withdrawal. This procedure has the added benefit of ecological validity, meaning it reflects circumstances that occur in infants' daily lives, because caregivers are routinely unable to pay attention to children as they would like, inadvertently signaling unavailability.

Behaviorally, infants typically respond to the SFP by looking away from the caregiver, smiling less, fussing and crying, and showing frustration or anger. More sustained negative responses (i.e., those lasting throughout the SFP and possibly into the recovery/reunion play episodes) reflect poor self-regulation, which has been shown to result in emotional and behavioral problems later in childhood. Physiologically, infants tend to display increases in heart rate and decreases in RSA, or vagal tone, described as a measure of the cardiac parasympathetic system, during a transition from play with the mother to the SFP. On the other hand, decreases in heart rate and increases in RSA from the SFP to a reunion with the mother (i.e., resumption of play) have been observed. These changes in vagal tone are of particular interest because RSA reactivity (i.e., decreases to the SFP and increases post–SFP) are thought to reflect a typical stress response: an adaptively functioning regulatory system that addresses stressors appropriately as they arise, related to executive functioning. It is important to note that different patterns have been observed in infants living in high-risk contexts, such as those with mothers who used substances or were of low socioeconomic status, making RSA work with infants even more compelling. Infants with less sensitive mothers display poorer heart rate recovery following repeated Still Face episodes, with a similar pattern found for infants prenatally exposed to cocaine and those born into family adversity (e.g., low socioeconomic status). According to some scholars, RSA can be considered a marker of the prefrontal cortex functioning responsible for executive attention and control—that is, a marker of a pathway that conveys information from the executive functions center in the brain to the body via a cardiovascular response.

Salivary cortisol concentrations, a psychobiological marker of the stress response, have also been measured in the SFP with infants. Overall, typically developing babies experience a rise in cortisol level during the still-face episodes and then a gradual decline after the reunion. Comparable to the heart rate and RSA findings, cortisol-level patterns also appear to vary in at-risk populations; specifically, increased infant cortisol levels post–SFP reunions have been observed in infants with less sensitive maternal care. Finally, infants in families affected by adversity (i.e., low Socioeconomic Status, maternal history of maltreatment and/or psychopathology, single-parent status) also show higher cortisol reactivity in response to the SFP. Interestingly, mothers with depression and a history of adversity who are resilient and engage in more positive parenting, responding more sensitively (i.e., identifying infant cues and responding appropriately), have infants with lower cortisol reactivity post–SFP.

Research with infants helps illustrate how brain and body systems interact to influence children's emotional reactions and regulation; that is, multiple brain and peripheral pathways provide the foundation for emotional and behavioral manifestations of temperament. Patterns of brain activity and network connections communicate with "downstream" processes, that is, those taking place in the rest of the body, directing physiological changes and subsequent overt expressions of emotional and motivational processes. The focus on the underlying neurobiological underpinnings may suggest that genetic mechanisms are responsible for this foundation of temperament styles and their intergenerational transmission. However, we should note that neurobiological systems are themselves open to environmental and social influences, starting with prenatal development, when maternal experiences can shape their growth.

TEMPERAMENT BEHAVIORS THAT STEM FROM BIOLOGY

Now that we have described the biological systems that underlie temperament we can better understand what temperament behaviors look like in different situations. For example, remember that crowded playground we mentioned in Chapter 1? Children with different temperament characteristics will not only respond differently to this situation, but they will actually experience it differently, some viewing it as threatening and others as delightful. A child who tends to be BIS dominant sees cues of danger and threat: "I could get hurt because the climber is too high." "I could get scared because the swings swing too high." "I might fall from the bridge; there are too many kids who might push me." "The kids might be mean to me or reject me." The cues of threat outshine the potential for reward. The child who tends to be BAS dominant sees, first and foremost, cues for potential reward and fun: "Climbing so high on the climber is thrilling." "I can feel like I'm flying because the swings swing so high." "I can jump on the bridge." "There are a lot of kids I can play with; some of them might be fun."

High-BIS children will likely stay by their parents or want their parents to take them to the playground and stand next to them. They might refuse to play on the playground altogether, foregoing the possibility of fun in exchange for safety. For a parent, you know your child tends to be safe, so you can worry less about them. At the same time, though, you might be concerned that they won't take advantage of a fun opportunity and may be missing out. High-BAS children might dive in, having fun on the playground and with other kids. But it might also mean they ran out of the car and across the parking lot because they couldn't wait to play. It might mean they are less careful while playing, for example, going down the slide before the child who went earlier has gotten off. Finally, some children will be able to modulate their initial or instinctive reaction through their higher levels of self-regulation, being able to overcome their desire to withdraw or approach, to do what one is supposed to do at a playground: have fun and be safe!

Some children might have high BIS or BAS reactivity, but they also might have a good capacity for managing their emotional reactions. For some, that might happen through their effortful or executive control abilities, and for others it might be through their efficient or effective self-soothing that arises from RSA or HPA system regulation. In appreciating your child's reactivity and self-regulation, it is useful to understand how these different capacities contribute. In the upcoming chapters, we talk more about these distinct emotional and behavioral patterns that arise from our neurobiological systems and temperament and how we can react to these most optimally as parents.

CONCLUSION

We hope that, after reading this chapter, you may view interactions with your child in a different light given the new information about the biological underpinnings of temperament, including brain–behavior connections and peripheral physiological processes that play important roles. This understanding should help you "pick your battles" and be more effective in the ones you choose to pursue, so that you are not fighting against biology underlying temperament traits but rather helping your child channel these in a more adaptive manner. Of course, knowing about emotion lateralization, for example, is not going to magically resolve every disagreement or power struggle; instead, this is something you can reflect on as you are being mindful of your goals when approaching challenging situations with your child, something that can help you interpret their behavior in a nonjudgmental manner, supporting a positive parenting response.

CHAPTER 4

CORE PARENTING PRINCIPLES

There is more than enough parenting advice available in the media, books, and online. Sometimes the advice is contradictory. For example, experts disagree about whether a child's allowance should be tied to things such as doing chores or good grades, or whether children should even have an allowance. Another example is whether parents should use time-outs with children. It has been called abusive by some, and yet there are years of research indicating that, when used appropriately, time outs can reduce problem behaviors. The plethora and range of advice can lead to confusion for any parent.

Even the best parenting advice assumes a one-size-fits-all approach to parenting. Some advice might not fit a family's culture or values or lifestyle. Also, many parents try recommended strategies and find that they don't work for them or their children, or they find that what worked with one child didn't work with the other. One reason for this might be because our children's temperament leads them to react differently to parenting strategies, and they might need a different approach.

In this chapter, we describe the parenting behaviors that are most often associated with positive social, emotional, and behavioral development. We discuss these further in Part II of this book, and in Part III we provide a toolkit of practices for engaging in these parenting behaviors. Overall, we're not advocates of a one-size-fits-all approach to parenting. Neither are we prescribing specific parenting behaviors for specific temperament styles. Instead, we are offering some general, core parenting principles along with some suggested strategies or steps parents can take in all parenting interactions. In the coming chapters, we talk about parenting strategies that parents can emphasize with children to match their temperament, providing what has been referred to in the temperament literature as *goodness-of-fit*. This is a powerful idea that speaks to the fact that parents can make adjustments in their approach to the child, ensuring that their demands, expectations, and support are appropriate for their child's temperament profile. In Part III of the book we offer specific exercises and practices for each core parenting principle.

In this chapter, we present some core guiding principles for parents that can be readily adapted to fit with different family cultures and values and with your child's temperament. Years of parenting research consistently point to a few key parenting behaviors that support children's social, emotional, and behavioral well-being. We have organized these into four core parenting principles: Be Present, Be Warm, Be Balanced, and Be Consistent.

BE PRESENT

Being mindful in parenting can support parents to be more attuned to and connected with their children and more effective in managing children's behaviors. *Mindfulness* is being present in the moment, with mind, heart, and body. It means bringing our attention to the moment intentionally and without judging or assuming. Mindfulness helps us to be more present, patient, calm, effective, and wise as we navigate our children's challenging behaviors and as we figure out what parenting practices work best for our children's unique temperament. Being present also provides situational awareness so that we can read our children better, such as knowing when giving the child an instruction to clean their room is going to be met with lesser or greater resistance, and knowing our own limitations, for example, stepping away from rule enforcement to regain composure after a stressful day at work.

BE WARM

Warmth refers to parents accepting their children for who they are and showing them affection and enjoyment. We don't use the word *love* for this because we know that parents love their children and would do anything for them. We use the term *warmth* because it captures the emotional quality of our relationships with our children. We recognize that there is no one way parents show their love and that warmth is just one specific way of doing so.

Warmth involves communicating acceptance of your child for who they are, appreciating through words and actions, their interests, personalities, and quirks. It includes enjoying being with your child and communicating to them their qualities that you appreciate. Parents who are higher in warmth will be lower in rejection; that is, they will less often criticize or mock their children's interests or personalities, be annoyed, or pick on little annoyances, and less often convey that their children are a nuisance. They will not try to change who their child is or their child's interests. Parents who show warmth and acceptance will more often point out their enjoyment and pride in their children. Warmth is also about being there to support and comfort your child as needed and showing them that you are interested in and care about their experiences and emotions.

Research has consistently shown that parenting that is characterized by greater warmth and acceptance and less rejection and criticism is associated with better social competence, emotion regulation, and academic competence in children. It is also related to lower anxiety and depressive symptoms and fewer behavior problems such as oppositional and aggressive behaviors. Warmth also reduces the likelihood of children developing problems when families experience stress and adversity. It is important to clarify that acceptance of who your child is does not mean approval of all of their behaviors, and a positive emotional tone is not always appropriate when children violate important rules or cross boundaries that have been firmly established. These problematic behaviors generally need to be acknowledged with some related consequences to follow, which we discuss in the "Be Consistent" section.

BE BALANCED

Being *balanced* in our parenting refers to being able to recognize and respond to our children's needs in a way that they need us to respond. This can be a balance of intervening or letting go, stepping in and stepping back (see Chapter 11). To do this in a way that is effective, we need to be aware of our children's emotions and needs. There are two main parenting behaviors that are involved in being balanced: responsiveness and scaffolding.

Responsive parenting is when parents are aware of their children's emotions and needs, and they respond in a way that addresses those needs. This involves being sensitive to cues our children give us about how they are feeling, even if they don't have words to tell us what they need. Cues can be found in our children's facial expressions, body language, emotions, and in their words. Responsiveness also involves having responses that are contingent on and relevant to our children's needs. *Contingency* means that we offer our children the support or solution when they actually need it, in response to their cues, not randomly, and not when we feel like it because of convenience or because certain responses make us feel good as parents. And *relevant* responses are those that actually address the child's need or emotion at the time.

An example of responsiveness is how a parent responds to an infant crying. Infants cry for any need or emotion—when they are hungry, tired, bored, uncomfortable, in pain, and so on. If a parent tries to feed a tired baby or put a hungry baby to sleep, they are trying to respond to the crying, but the response does not address the child's need and usually makes things worse.

Responsiveness means being sensitive to our children's cues, discerning their needs, and responding appropriately and consistently. This can be challenging when we also take into account our children's developmental level and temperament, and sometimes the needs cannot be readily addressed, such as when a tired child cries because they want to go home, but you are in the middle of an appointment or travel, making going home impossible at the moment. In these situations, responsiveness is nurturance in the face of distress, and it takes a lot of composure to respond to a crying child calmly when we ourselves may be feeling stressed. Responsiveness together with warmth has been shown to support children's secure attachment to, or bond with, their caregivers, better emotion regulation, and cognitive development, and it can mitigate the effects of stress and adversity on children's developmental outcomes.

Scaffolding—in essence, coaching—involves parents' encouragement of autonomy and independence balanced with just the right amount of guidance, structure, or instruction. This type of coaching is supportive and growth oriented rather than critical and punitive. Scaffolding is particularly applicable to situations when children are learning something new, facing a challenging social situation, trying to solve a problem, or dealing with a difficult emotion. This is a challenging parenting skill because we want to offer just enough, but not too much, support. It is dynamic and requires knowing when to step in, when to step back to allow autonomy, and when to allow our children to struggle a little as they are learning something new or dealing with a challenging situation. Research suggests that children learn best when they have the opportunity to be successful 85% of the time and have the chance to struggle or fail 15% of the time (Blue, 2019). We want to step in to provide support so our children can be successful about 85% of the time, but we want to make sure they have a chance to try, struggle, and maybe fail about 15% of the time.

Thinking of scaffolding in the form of coaching, or music instruction, is helpful. During practices, the coach or instructor is teaching the skill, providing instruction and guidance, and structuring the lesson. However, during a game or performance the coach is on the sideline, and the instructor is off to the side. The child is center stage, performing and applying the skills they learned and learning from mistakes they make. Scaffolding is particularly important in supporting children's developing self-regulation and cognitive and academic skills. A related parenting behavior—*emotion coaching*, which is specific to scaffolding children's emotional experiences, responses, and behaviors—supports better emotional awareness and regulation.

BE CONSISTENT

Consistency, or consistent limit setting, refers to providing children with clear, reasonable, and age-appropriate expectations for their behaviors and rules around undesirable behaviors. A family might expect that members are respectful of and helpful toward each other, and these expectations have implications for child behavior, for example, defining name-calling or hitting as unacceptable. Consistency also refers to having established contingencies that both reinforce desirable behaviors and discourage unacceptable behaviors. For example, privileges such as playing with friends or media time might be contingent on the child meeting family expectations regarding being respectful and helpful, and consequences would be imposed when unacceptable behaviors occur.

Consequences can be natural, such as cleaning up after making a mess or breaking something, or logical, such as temporarily losing a toy or a privilege for hitting a sibling to get the toy. Most important, contingencies should be consistent and predictable. If they are sometimes applied and sometimes not applied, it can create confusion and increase conflict and opposition. For some children, it also creates a sense that it might be worth trying to break a rule if sometimes they can get away with it. For example, if playing a video game before completing chores is sometimes punished and sometimes allowed, your child might try to get away with it even if they know it's against the family rules.

Consistent limit setting is related to better social competence, self-regulation, and fewer behavior problems such as oppositional and aggressive behaviors. It is also related to lower anxiety and depression symptoms in children. This might be because it creates a predictable and understandable family environment that allows children to have a sense of control and agency in their lives.

In Appendix B we include a tool that will allow you to reflect on your own parenting behaviors. This will allow you to get a sense of where your parenting falls within a range on each of the dimensions described in this chapter.

CONCLUSION

We encourage parents to think about their parenting in terms of being present, warm, balanced, and consistent. Being present in the moment in our interactions with our children, and observing without judging or criticizing, allows us to be mindful, calm, and wise as parents. Being warm means that we accept and enjoy our children, showing them delight and affection. Being balanced allows us to respond to our children's emotions and needs in the way they need us to while we also provide a balance of guidance, structure, and autonomy. This maximizes our children's opportunities to learn and build skills. Finally, by being consistent, providing clear, reasonable, and age-appropriate expectations and rules, parents can create a sense of predictability, control, and security for their children.

Although all children benefit from parents who are present, warm, balanced, and consistent, parents can tailor their parenting to their children's temperament characteristics, using different tools or emphasizing different behaviors to be more effective. In Part II of this book we delve into specific temperament characteristics and share which parenting approaches are effective with each characteristic.

II

PARENTING WITH YOUR CHILD'S TEMPERAMENT IN MIND

CHAPTER 5

THE FEARFUL OR FEARLESS CHILD

When my (Liliana's) oldest daughter was 2 1/2, I enrolled her in a dance class at our community center. It was an 8-week class taught by a warm and welcoming ballet instructor. My daughter was excited about dancing, but when we arrived at class she clung to me and asked to leave. I have known since she was born that she is a more reactive child (she has stronger emotional reactions than most), and I also knew she was pretty fearful in unfamiliar situations. Instead of leaving, we sat through the whole class with her on my lap. I encouraged her to join the class, but she declined, and I didn't push her. I just let her watch. The next week we attended, she again refused to join the class. Instead of sitting with her in my lap, we sat on the floor. The next week was the same, except I had her sit a couple of feet in front of me. The next week was the same, but I had her sit halfway between me and the circle of dancers. The next week, she joined the circle, but didn't dance. This went on until the last week of class, when she pulled off her leggings (I don't know why!) and danced with the class. She had been obviously paying attention because she knew what to do. She also continued dancing with the same instructor for the next 2 years, and rarely refused to enter another class again, even though she often had trepidation about doing so.

Other parents of children who express frequent or intense fear reactions to novelty or uncertainty likely had similar experiences, maybe not with a dance class but with swimming lessons or switching to a new day care or preschool. Children who are moderately high in fear are also sometimes referred to as "slow to warm up." My daughter's experience with her first dance class is a good illustration of how this term came into use. Over time, with persistent exposure (i.e., continued attendance at dance lessons), children are able to engage in the previously feared activity in a meaningful way. In this chapter we delve into the temperament dimension of fear, starting with children at the higher end of the continuum, that is, children who are more fearful, and the risk as well as protection this higher level of fear affords. We specifically focus on how higher levels of child fearful reactivity present in interactions with parents, how parents tend to react, and approaches that can be most effective for children high in fear. Next, we turn to those on the low end of this characteristic, that is, fearless children, also emphasizing challenges and opportunities in the parent–child relationship.

FEARFUL CHILDREN

As we discussed in Chapters 2 and 3, fearful children are easily unsettled by novel, ambiguous, or uncertain situations, often clinging, crying, whining, and throwing temper tantrums when confronted with the unfamiliar or the unexpected. Fear is definitely unpleasant, because it comes with a negative emotional state and uncomfortable physiological experiences (e.g., escalation in heart rate, changes in breathing, gastrointestinal distress). In the next sections, we describe the causes and consequences of fear, how parents and children interact when a child is high in fear, and what parenting approaches are effective.

Causes and Consequences of Being Fearful

Fear stems from our flight response, in which we are attuned to potential threats or negative consequences and try to avoid them. Not surprisingly, there is a strong motivation to avoid things, people, and situations that elicit fearful responses; however, this avoidance motivation can become problematic because, as noted earlier, really fearful children tend to fear relatively minor, ordinary situations that other children their age tolerate with ease. For example, it most likely is not possible to avoid going to preschool because there is unfamiliar equipment in the classroom, or not feasible to forego visiting grandparents on holidays because unfamiliar relatives tend to show up unexpectedly. Nathan Fox and colleagues (Fox, 1994; Fox & Pine, 2012) have proposed that children who go on to experience anxiety symptoms or disorders as a consequence of extreme fearfulness are more likely to detect and focus on any novel or potentially threatening information in a situation and react to it by avoiding the situation: an automatic form of control, rather than the effortful, flexible attention-based regulation we have discussed.

Moderate levels of fearfulness are generally adaptive, alerting us to dangerous situations. According to some work by Grazyna Kochanska (1993; Kochanska & Knaack, 2003), moderate levels of fearfulness are even conducive to development of self-regulation; however, extremely high levels can result in a cascade of developmental effects that often lead to anxiety and depression. Intensive studies that followed infants over time, and sometimes into adulthood, have shown that infants who react strongly to novelty become toddlers who hesitate to approach unfamiliar objects and people and later struggle with unfamiliar peers in preschool or kindergarten (Kagan & Snidman, 2009). Part of this stability of the fearful temperament is thought to come from the underlying pattern of brain activity, specifically, brain activity lateralized predominantly to the right hemisphere in the frontal region. In fact, Cynthia Smith and Martha Ann Bell (2010) showed that stability in greater relative right frontal activation across infancy predicted anxiety- and depression-related symptoms in preschoolers. It is important to note, though, that whether high levels of fearful reactivity are maintained over time or turn into an anxiety or depressive disorder is determined by multiple factors. The relationships children have with parents, caregivers, and teachers can be the most important of these.

How Fearful Children Respond to Their Parents

Because fearful children tend to see threatening cues in their environment and will often try to avoid threatening or aversive situations, they are also likely to be good at learning and following expectations and rules. These are children who may need to be told only once not to run into the street because it's dangerous, or not to get out of their seat in class because they will get in trouble. Their fear of a negative consequence usually makes them pretty good at following the expectations of the adults around them. This can be true until fearful children are really afraid of something, and they dig in their heels, refusing to do it. At these times, it is incredibly difficult for the child to do what their parent or teacher is asking them to do. They can so strongly oppose the request or expectation that they can become oppositional, angry, belligerent, or maybe even aggressive. With peers, more fearful children tend to be slower to make new friends, but once they have friends they are careful not to provoke anger, often developing good skills for navigating relationships. Of course, some assertiveness can be helpful in managing peer relationships, and standing up for oneself may cause friends to become angry, so parents need to be ready to offer some support in managing conflict.

Another behavioral challenge can arise if the fearful child's compliance is motivated by a fear of displeasing adults and the potential consequences of that, rather than developing an internalized understanding of the reasons for the adult's expectations. When this is the case, some parents see a shift in their fearful children as the children enter preadolescence and adolescence. It is in this developmental transition that peers start to increase in their importance in the child's world. The motivation to avoid incurring their peers' rejection might overtake the motivation to avoid their parents' or other adults' displeasure. This might lead children to be more oppositional, violating their parents' rules and expectations. Given this, parents want to be aware of their young children's motivations for complying—are they fearful of the parent's displeasure with them, or are they internalizing the reasons for the rules? If parents lean on the first motivation, then they will likely face challenges later.

How Parents Respond to Fearful Children

Children who are fearful tend to elicit two kinds of responses from parents. The first is a protective, comforting response. When a fearful child looks terrified of walking into a friend's birthday party, it is almost instinctive for a parent to offer comfort and protection. In fact, parents are biologically programmed to respond to a fearful facial expression with a protective response, even when the parent knows that the birthday party is not a dangerous context. However, responding protectively also sends the child a message that, in fact, the child needs to be protected, reinforcing the fearful response. The second common response to a child who is overly fearful can be frustration and anger. Parents, teachers, or coaches can be annoyed with the response when the child is withdrawing from or avoiding a situation that is clearly safe. Pushing the child to enter the situation, becoming frustrated or angry, or making critical comments can make the child feel worse about themselves and about the situation. Either response, the overprotective response or the critical response, tends to actually increase a child's fearfulness. This means that the most effective way through these situations is a balanced, middle way. Parenting a child who is fearful requires a careful balance of support and validation coupled with gentle but firm encouragement to approach the feared experience, which we discuss later in this chapter.

As you can imagine, for parents who are themselves fearful their instinct will be to protect their child, because they might relate to the child's experience or even themselves see the situation as threatening. For parents who are more fearless or who are easily frustrated, their response might be to criticize or push the child too strongly because they are not able to relate to the fearful response. Sometimes, parents differ in their own temperaments, so one parent is inclined to empathize with the child's fearful reactions, offering protection, whereas the other parent sees the child's fearfulness as an overreaction to an objectively safe situation, becoming frustrated. Of course, there are many times when parents can and should agree to disagree. However, having vastly different approaches to intense fear reactions can further exacerbate the problem, and parents who cannot agree on a balanced middle way could benefit from consultation with a child mental health provider or developmental specialist.

What Works Best With Fearful Children?

With a better understanding of the motivations, emotions, and behaviors often seen in children who are higher in fearfulness, we now turn to specific recommendations for parenting more effectively with a fearful child. We describe how matching parental expectations and behaviors to the unique aspects of this temperament trait can help mitigate typical challenges, helping fearful children manage exposure to novelty or uncertainty and promote their well-being.

Balance Support With Structure

Early in infancy, responding to the child in a sensitive manner across the board is certainly appropriate and conducive to a number of positive outcomes, such as secure attachment. Children of parents who respond to infant cues promptly and appropriately develop a sense of security, wherein they seek proximity to the parent so they will feel safe when sensing potential danger (e.g., unfamiliar adults approaching), and they are able to explore the environment further away from a caregiver when not feeling threatened. However, toward the end of the first year of life and in the toddler period, the buffering afforded by indiscriminate sensitivity wanes and, at least for some children, there is corresponding risk.

According to Kristin Buss and others (e.g., Buss & Kiel, 2011, 2013), consistently sensitive responding, especially during times of distress, may lead to greater behavioral inhibition (hesitation to approach new things, people, and situations) and an increased risk of anxiety for children already high in fearfulness. It is thought that such sensitivity may serve to accommodate avoidance, in turn maintaining and potentially escalating fearful behaviors. Moreover, when caregivers move in quickly to attempt to alleviate child distress they may miss providing important opportunities for their children to learn to self-soothe, distract their attention, and lower their own level of arousal. In other words, children of parents who are sensitive to distress and quick to intervene may miss important opportunities to develop and practice self-regulation skills in fear-eliciting situations.

Accommodation of child fear and avoidance also results in missed opportunities for skill and competence building, such as when a fearful child does not participate in activities that are not familiar or comfortable, for example, trying out a new sport or hobby or avoiding birthday parties and sleepovers. Starting in the preschool period, children develop sufficient self-awareness and social comparison accuracy that they understand when their avoidance is not consistent with what same-age peers are typically doing (i.e., that they are becoming age inappropriate), and their self-concept can suffer as a result, also increasing the risk of depression if they regularly think, "I am not as good as other kids because . . .". In this situation, children benefit from validation, and we discuss validation skills in Chapter 10.

Be Gentle, Firm, and Consistent

Of course, not accommodating a fearful child who is motivated to avoid novel or ambiguous situations doesn't mean just forcing them to do things they would ordinarily prefer to skip. In fact, parents of children who are on the fearful end of the spectrum are most effective when they use gentle, firm discipline; are generally responsive; and make use of gentle exposure. As noted, parents can feel especially protective of these children. However, overprotectiveness leads to indulgence of avoidant behavior, wherein a more uncomfortable or "risky" choice is never made. Instead, preparation for a novel situation and guidance to stick with the plan even if things seem uncomfortable or awkward will likely lead to "baby steps" in the direction of greater exposure to the unfamiliar (e.g., social events with peers). Of course, this becomes easier with older children who can engage in conversations about planning and coping with discomfort in a meaningful way. But even toddlers who are beginning to master language (comprehension is generally more advanced than expressive language at this time) can be engaged in discussions about dangerous versus uncomfortable. This theme is very important for a fearful child and should be repeated across contexts—"It's OK to feel uncomfortable; it's not the same thing as being in danger. . . . Sometimes you have to be uncomfortable for a little while; what's awkward now will become familiar." As this approach is practiced, you will develop more and more examples to turn to, such as "Remember how going to gymnastics was awkward at first, and now you love it and know everyone at the gym." See Chapter 12 for tips about being consistent.

Be Calm

Approaches that will definitely not lead to desired results involve yelling and power-assertive discipline. Loud speech, negative comments, and confrontational body language only serve to frighten fearful children more, further disrupting their ability to regulate their emotions. It is important for parents to keep their cool, take their own time-out if needed, so that they do not raise their voice and start threatening or saying things they would not be uttering if they were more regulated and planning what to say. We remind parents that supporting fearful children to overcome their avoidance and anxiety requires carefully balancing warm support and validation with gentle and consistent limit-setting. This is challenging for any parent. Parents might benefit from understanding and using the Wise Mind practice we describe in Chapter 9, asking yourself, "What is needed? And what will be effective for my child in this situation?" Also in Chapter 9, we provide some practices and tools for building our own self-regulation to help navigate this challenge; these include Paced Breathing, STOP, Wise Mind, and Parent Time-Out.

FEARLESS CHILDREN

As noted earlier, fearless children represent the other end of the temperament spectrum, with different underlying neurophysiology (i.e., relative left frontal dominance). Developmentally, fearless children are not disturbed by novelty as infants, showing interest in unfamiliar adults and activities, for example, eagerly interacting with strangers in line at the supermarket or wanting to go onto climbing equipment that seems too advanced in terms of required motor skills.

Causes and Consequences of Being Fearless

Accommodation or harsh parental responses might also be prompted by fearless children, but for very different reasons. These approaches will also not be effective with a fearless child, although with these children, who are seemingly not intimidated by threat or danger, parents often feel at their wits' end for other reasons. As toddlers and preschoolers, these children become more challenging because they now have greater access to more potentially dangerous situations, such as crossing the street. Because, for fearless children, behavioral inhibition does not provide a conduit to self-regulation, parents and other care providers and educators find themselves working harder to support these skills. Fearless children are not inherently motivated to slow down and process information when any cues interpreted as potential signs of danger are detected, which is what fearful children are inclined to do. These cues are simply not prioritized for processing in fearless children, and as a result they are often missed and/or do not play the typical inhibitory role, so behavior is not interrupted.

How Fearless Children Respond to Their Parents

Fearless children do not hesitate to jump into an activity that looks like fun, which can be very enjoyable for the whole family when playing games, trying a new sport, going to an amusement park, and so on. When these types of activities are presented, children who are extremely low in fearful reactivity are typically immediately excited and enthusiastic about participating. As long as there is little opportunity for risk taking, parents can likely relax and have fun as well.

However, when danger lurks and risky choices can be made, fearless children can be a challenge because they often forget parents' instructions about safety, or they don't follow them because they are so enticed by the exciting activity. Sometimes this happens because parents lecture about potential risk and dangers, providing too much information and failing to prioritize key information. Young fearless children continue to pursue the desired activity without much regard for limits being set on them, and they may simply verbalize something like "No," indicating they are not going to conform to parental expectations regarding safety. When older fearless children respond to parental guidance and prohibitions, these verbal responses are often dismissive, not conforming to parental instructions. Remember, these children are not really afraid of getting in trouble or of the negative consequences parents have outlined for undesirable or unsafe behaviors, so warnings about those tend to have little impact on their behavior. Better regulated fearless children may learn to listen and plan on complying when parental instructions are provided, but then forget all about this important guidance once the desired activity begins and they experience a sense of fun and enjoyment.

How Parents Respond to Fearless Children

From the parents' perspective, the fact that severely limited fear reactivity does not slow these children down in dangerous situations is most concerning. As long as a situation involves a potentially rewarding element, such as excitement generated by jumping off rocks or bridges into the water, or skiing downhill really fast, accompanying dangerous elements will likely be overlooked by a fearless child. Of course, it can be perfectly safe to jump into water or go fast down a slope. The problem is that when one does not prioritize more dangerous elements for information processing (which is what happens with fearless children), decisions are likely made without taking potential dangers into consideration. So, there is little or no checking of water depth, no inclination to wear a life jacket or to check how steep a slope is before starting downhill. Thus, a lacking or a severely limited fear response can lead to unintended injuries, challenging parents in terms of limit-setting.

Parenting the fearless child requires that one find an appropriate balance among proactive guidance or scaffolding, firm boundaries, consistent limit-setting, and being warm and supportive. This can be very challenging. Such challenges arise primarily because the way fearless children react can make us feel like bad parents and as though the relationship we work so hard to maintain is not being valued. When there have been many conversations about safety, needing to stay close in public places—while shopping in an outdoor market, for example—and the fearless child darts away, disregarding all of it at the first opportunity, it is a defeating experience for any parent. The natural inclination is to say that all of that effort devoted to building a warm relationship and to providing guidance, reinforcing rules, and establishing boundaries has been wasted. However, it would be more helpful to reframe this experience as another illustration of the power of the fearless temperament. With that frame, parents can be more motivated to continue efforts to provide structure and encourage self-regulation and reflective thinking. It might also be a good idea to prepare a Plan B, for example, if there is an unintended separation in a public place.

What Works Best With Fearless Children?

Because fearless temperament bodes risk for noncompliance and aggression, which in turn have their own developmental consequences (e.g., academic difficulties, delinquency, and substance use), having a warm relationship, being responsive, and consistency in setting limits are critical. Although having a close and warm relationship will not always prevent a fearless child from taking a riskier route, it will be protective in the long run. When a child feels accepted and emotionally close to the parents, they are more likely to turn to them for guidance and support. As children grow, riskier choices turn from running into the street to getting involved with a so-called "deviant" peer group, with friends who break rules, get in trouble, use substances early, and engage in unsafe sexual behavior. When a child facing related choices feels close to caregivers, they are going to be more likely to talk about these and be more open to adult guidance (especially when it is communicated in a matter of fact, nonjudgmental manner). This is true for all children, but it can be especially protective for fearless children who often put themselves in riskier situations, because signs of danger are dismissed or minimized. At the same time, consistent and firm boundaries are needed for fearless youth, with clear messages about acceptable and unacceptable behaviors, for example, regarding the importance of coming home at an agreed-upon time and returning after curfew being unacceptable. Without fundamental rules that are reinforced with predictable and reliable consequences (e.g., "If you come home late, you will not be able to go out next weekend"), fearless children are likely to drift toward risky behaviors, even in the context of parental warmth and acceptance. No wonder finding an appropriate balance between proactive guidance/scaffolding, firm boundaries, consistent consequences, and being warm and supportive can be challenging with fearless children.

Be Warm

These children don't follow rules because they are not afraid of the consequences. Thus, having a warm, attuned relationship helps because it provides a foundation of mutual trust and respect. This foundation, in turn, makes it possible for a child to follow parental instructions even when they do not care about consequences per se but because the parent made it clear it is important to them that their child do what they are being asked to do to be safe. In other words, parents can get their relationship to work for them in seeking cooperation from a fearless child if this relationship is a warm and accepting one and if the child generally feels like their parents care about their needs, interests, and safety. Being warm and offering guidance should be frequent in typical interactions.

Sometimes parents get frustrated with their fearless children, finding it difficult to be warm and responsive. We provide information about practices parents can use to maintain a warm relationship with our children in Chapter 10. These include Active Listening, Child-Led Time, and Validation.

Provide Scaffolding

You may recall that responsiveness is one tool for being balanced. Responsiveness involves how we as parents and caregivers are able to identify children's needs and address these in a meaningful way. You may not feel like a particularly warm parent after you had to set yet another limit, or yet again enforce the same limit that is often challenged by your fearless child, but you are being warm and responsive when you work with your child to address their behavior. When you say things like, "Let's figure out what to do next . . ." or "I can help you fix this . . .," responsiveness is instrumental: It is aimed at solving problems. At the same time, responsive actions convey to your child that you are invested and attuned to their needs.

Fearless children also might benefit from having extra support, cues, and reminders around safety. Think about providing a lot of guidance and structuring. It is important to meet our children where they are in terms of offering these supports. It might not be enough to say "Be careful" in a situation it may instead be more helpful to identify the potential risks in a situation and how to handle them. This is easier to do when children are younger so they can start building these skills early. Think of this as coaching a skill. The coaching analogy helps parents envision how to do this. Think of a coach teaching children a sport for the first time. It starts with the most basic skills and lots of instruction and structure. As an individual gets better and better at the sport, the coach can step back and provide guidance and suggestions. For fearless children, parents would start with the most basic safety cues in a situation, highlighting them and helping the child notice and think about them. This should be a warm, positive teaching opportunity. If it is negative or harsh, the fearless child will most likely tune out. We provide more information about scaffolding in Chapter 11.

Be Consistent

Being clear and consistent when enforcing expectations, rules, or limits is incredibly important with fearless children. Cues about negative consequences or potential threats are not at the forefront of their minds. However, repetition and consistency of limits and consequences helps make the awareness of them a habit, in the same way that practicing a skill over and over can make the skill automatic. In Chapter 12, we provide some guidelines and tools, including the Precise Directions tool, for developing a consistent contingency plan. When limits have to be enforced, or consequences are warranted, more concise communication works best; parents should stick to a script that reiterates the rules and consequences they deem appropriate.

CONCLUSION

The temperament dimension of fear is unique compared with the others we discuss in this book in that both very high and very low levels can present challenges for parents. However, the challenges are very different and require parents to tailor their parenting in different ways to be effective.

Children who are high in fearfulness react to meeting unfamiliar people or being in unfamiliar situations by avoiding or withdrawing and experiencing feelings of anxiety and, if pushed to do something they don't want to do, they can react with defiance or tantrums. Parents sometimes respond by either overprotecting and accommodating children's fears or with anger and frustration. Either response can increase children's fearfulness over time. To support fearful children in reducing the extent to which their fear drives their behaviors, parents can build a warm, positive relationship with their children, building trust so that when they gently encourage and scaffold feared activities children are more likely to try things. This requires parents to be gentle, firm, and consistent. It also requires parents to be aware of and manage their own emotional reactions to their children. Conversations that make distinctions between things and situations that are objectively dangerous versus those that feel uncomfortable or awkward can also be helpful to children, with the point being that being uncomfortable does not equal danger. With older children, who are more advanced in their understanding of probabilities, you can also talk about certain things being probable and others only being possible, and so very unlikely to occur. Such discussions should not occur during already-tense moments, and discussions alone will not make a fearful child more eager to engage with the new and unfamiliar. However, they can help provide a foundation or context for children understanding their own reactions and enhancing coping skills. With these efforts, both parents and children will have more opportunities to enjoy new experiences and each other, and parents can appreciate that their children can approach their life with a balance of caution and joy.

Children who are very low in fear are usually enthusiastic and excited about diving into a situation, and parents can enjoy their children's delight and energy. However, fearless children are also less likely to see the risks or dangers in a situation. This makes them more likely to engage in risky behaviors, especially if they are also low in self-regulation. For parents, this can be scary, in particular when typical warnings about safety do not seem to work. Being effective with fearless children requires an appropriate balance between proactive guidance and structuring of a situation, firm boundaries, consistent limit-setting, and being warm and supportive. Although this sounds similar to the approach used with fearful children, the specific things parents do are rather different. For example, when approaching a playground with tall play equipment and multiple children, a fearful child would benefit from parental warmth and responsiveness and, most of all, encouragement to engage with reminders about potential fun. On the other hand, a parent of a fearless child would be best advised to discuss boundaries and limitations—"Keep your hands to yourself," "Wait for other children to be done before going down the slide,"—possibly reminding them to "Follow these rules, or we will have to leave." At the same time, one parallel approach should be noted: Parents of children on both ends of the continuum will be most effective if they are consistent in their efforts. Consistency is so critical because it ensures that your child is exposed to as many learning opportunities as possible. For example, when you always insist that your child accept birthday party invitations and attend, because birthdays are important, a highly fearful child will come to accept associated discomfort. In addition, when you practice an approach only occasionally—for example, only sometimes demand that your child leave the playground after they failed to abide by safety rules—it is not clear to your child that this is important, something they really need to attend to.

It can be helpful to have conversations about the lessons and values you are trying to instill, such as "It is important to try new things" or "Think before you act," when you are not in the midst of a challenging situation, when things are calm and everyone feels good. Also, don't forget to notice and enjoy your children's successes, when, for example, they go to an event they were hoping to avoid without argument, or take their time in choosing the best route for their first ride on a new bike. A new parenting approach may not initially come naturally, or it can seem awkward when first attempted. Just like anything else, the more you practice it, the more comfortable it will become over time.

CHAPTER 6

THE EASILY FRUSTRATED CHILD

One day, my (Liliana's) son was particularly angry because I wasn't letting him do something he wanted to do. He yelled at me, "You are so mean!" He then stormed down the hallway to his room and slammed the door. The frustration genes run on my side of the family, so, when confronted with his anger, I was pretty upset, but when he slammed the door something inside me snapped. I stomped down the hall, opened his door and yelled, "You are not allowed to slam the door!" Then, I slammed the door. I stood with my hand on the doorknob, instantly aware of my hypocrisy, when a couple of seconds later, my son yelled from behind the door, "You just slammed the door!"

Most of us have heard it—our children calling us mean because we won't let them do something they want to do. Or they storm down the hall and slam the door because they didn't get what they wanted. All children experience frustration and anger, for lots of reasons, but the most common sources of frustration are being blocked in our attempt to achieve a goal or get what we want, or when we feel attacked, confronted, or threatened by someone else's anger. However, for some children the feelings of frustration and anger erupt more readily, over little things, and sometimes intensely and out of proportion to the situation.

For example, in a family I (Liliana) once worked with in my clinical practice, the younger of their two sons, who were 1 year apart in age, was often angry and yelling at his parents, blowing up unexpectedly. He sometimes became destructive around the house. It was puzzling to the parents to have two sons behave so differently when they were close in age and equally intelligent, attractive, and athletic and who were equally loved and supported by the parents. They lived in the same house, with the same parents, under the same expectations and rules. The older son was calm and responsive to his parents' directions, generally following their rules even if he didn't like them. The younger son was hot-headed, becoming angry when he didn't get what he wanted or when people contradicted him. Of course, there could be a lot of different family dynamics going on here, but from my work with them it appeared that this was largely a temperament difference between the boys, and it was puzzling to the parents how the boys could react so differently to basically similar parenting and family experiences. What worked with one son didn't work with the other because one of the boys had a more difficult time, that is, stronger negative emotional reactions, with goals being blocked or rewards being absent or removed.

CAUSES AND CONSEQUENCES OF BEING EASILY FRUSTRATED

As noted, frustration generally arises from barriers to our efforts to go after something we want. It stems from activation in the behavioral activation system, and when children are easily frustrated it is likely because they are a high–behavioral activation system or approach- and reward-oriented person with a highly reactive defense system (fight–flight system), discussed in Chapter 3. Children who are easily or intensely frustrated grow angry quickly, and sometimes at little things. They can react angrily to being told it's time to stop playing a game or time to go to bed. They can argue about eating something they don't want to eat or about not getting to eat something they do want to eat. Their frustration can flare up when they are contradicted or disagree with a peer or sibling because they can feel confronted or attacked. They are likely to become flooded with anger and not think clearly, saying or doing things that inflame or exacerbate a situation and others around them rather than doing something effective to get what they want.

Children who are high in frustration reactivity are more likely to have a number of social, emotional, and behavioral problems. This doesn't mean they all have difficulties, but they have a greater likelihood of problems, especially when their experiences or contexts are stressful, exacerbate their frustration, or don't address their frustration appropriately. Children who are highly and easily frustrated can have problems with peers, showing fewer skills in peer interactions, often getting in arguments or fights with peers and generally struggling to make or keep friends. They can be easily provoked to anger so might be more likely to be picked on by others. As a result, there tends to be higher levels of aggressive behaviors among these children. Easily frustrated children are also more oppositional with adults. They are more likely to disobey or argue when a parent or teacher gives a directive. This might be because they don't want to stop what they are doing, or they don't want to do what they are being asked. But unlike other children in the same situation, their frustration or anger is aroused, and it interferes with them acting effectively or adapting to the demands of the situation. Children who are highly and easily frustrated are also more likely to show signs of depression, perhaps because their relationships with adults and peers are problematic and because they start to feel bad about themselves and their lives.

However, keep in mind that these are probabilities, and not all children who are easily frustrated develop these problems. Some of these potential outcomes depend on how the adults and contexts around the children handle excessive frustration. When parents and other adults can cultivate a warm, accepting relationship with these children; maintain consistency in setting limits; and regulate their own negative, harsh, and angry responses; highly and easily frustrated children usually do just fine and over time learn to manage their reactivity more effectively themselves. This can be accomplished if we do not take our children's anger and frustration personally. It is not that they are disrespecting us as parents but instead that their biologically based, easily frustrated temperament is getting the better of them. Of course, parents do feel disrespected when their children yell, and this is when understanding the temperamental foundations of emotionally charged behavior can play an important role in helping us respond more effectively.

Given that adults' responses can make a difference in the developmental outcomes for these children, understanding how parents react to easily frustrated children, how children respond differently to their parents, and how parents can work most effectively with these children is critically important. For parents who are easily frustrated themselves, managing a calm and thought-out response to a child's excessive frustration may be particularly challenging. Mindfulness can be helpful in these situations, and cultivating a more mindful approach to parenting would likely be beneficial. In Chapter 9, we suggest some ways to help you practice mindfulness.

Let's also point out the wonderful aspects of being a child who is easily frustrated. Recall that a lot of that frustration reactivity stems from being blocked from something they want or are enjoying, or being made to do something they don't want to do. Most of the time, we can all learn a lesson from these children about really, deeply enjoying the things we are doing and feeling passionately about the little enjoyable things in our lives—playing, having a cookie, or wearing comfortable pajamas. Imagine if we all relished a little more in the everyday joys and pleasures of our lives. These children can be strongly invested in things that they enjoy, so their interests and passions can be encouraged fairly easily. For parents, being able to relish their children's passion and enjoyment, while navigating the frustration and anger effectively, can lead to a very close relationship founded on shared interests and emotional experiences. It's important to be mindful of the fact that your relationship with your child is not just about instances of frustrations and management of anger—at least, it should not be, so you might need to figure out ways to spend quality time together, doing the things your child really wants to do.

HOW EASILY FRUSTRATED CHILDREN RESPOND TO THEIR PARENTS

Children who are easily frustrated respond to their parents differently than other children. They are quick to anger and can respond with anger even in situations that aren't initially confrontational because they can read threat or criticism in situations even when they weren't intended. Their responses can be intense, so that parents don't know what hit them when their children start throwing a fit. When children are old enough to talk, they are old enough to start arguing, and easily frustrated children can be argumentative about every little thing. Easily frustrated children are more likely to respond to a parent's directions or requests by being oppositional, refusing to do what they are being asked. I (Liliana) remember when my son was young, and I would ask him to do something he didn't want to do. He would walk down the hallway yelling, "No, I don't want to; I'm not going to," as he was going to do the thing I asked him to do. He knew that he would have to do it eventually, anyway, because we learned to be very consistent in enforcing our expectations of him, as we discuss later. But he would often argue and be frustrated the whole time he did what was asked. Regardless, we made sure to communicate our appreciation that he did what was asked.

Easily frustrated children are also more likely to lash out physically or with aggression, shrugging or jerking away if you take their arm, hitting if they feel constrained or cornered. This happens more often when they are younger and less able to express themselves verbally. But even older children find themselves tongue-tied with anger and respond physically in some way, such as throwing something, hitting the table, or slamming a door. Remember, their fight response system is activated when they feel threatened or challenged and their physiological response is telling them to fight. Parents' own responses can make a big difference for these children.

HOW PARENTS RESPOND TO EASILY FRUSTRATED CHILDREN

If any of this is familiar to you, then you will most likely also recognize that parents who have children who are highly and easily frustrated often respond in ways they are not proud of, like when I (Liliana) slammed the door on my son. It was not one of my best parenting moments. Parents who have children who are easily frustrated tend to respond to them with increasing levels of harsh, frustrated, angry, and negative behaviors themselves over time, contributing to the cycle of escalating negative and angry interactions. It may be stating the obvious to say that interacting with people who are highly and easily frustrated can be frustrating. These children tend to draw out the worst in our parenting, and we might find ourselves reacting in ways we never expected. These frustrated, angry, or negative reactions on our part can then contribute to a negative or escalating angry cycle in our relationships with our children. If you have an easily frustrated child, you might be accustomed to interactions that start out with a typical direction or request that elicits an angry response from your child and that you respond to with frustration, anger, or yelling. The prompts and reasoning that might work well with other children often don't work that well with easily frustrated children, and parents can feel like they are short on options for handling these situations constructively and effectively. In fact, to be effective with an easily frustrated child, a parent has to lay down a lot of preventative groundwork that we describe later in this chapter.

Parents also tend to use less reasoning over time, resorting instead to edicts and punishments for not listening. We know that interacting with children in a way that helps them understand the reasons for a rule or expectation, the impact on others for violating the rule or expectation, and the potential consequences if a child does so tends to lead to greater child compliance. However, parents grow less likely to use reasoning with children who are easily frustrated because it doesn't seem to work as well in shaping their behavior. For example, I might explain to my child that I don't want her to climb on the furniture because I don't want her to get hurt, and I don't want my furniture to get ruined. Many children upon being told they can't climb on the furniture will be disappointed but will understand the reasons and find something else to do. That doesn't mean they won't ever do it again, because they will. However, if a rule about not climbing on the furniture is consistently enforced, then eventually most children will follow that rule. However, with a high approach- and reward-oriented child, the allure of climbing on the furniture and the sheer pleasure of doing it often will override their judgment about complying with the family rule. When a parent (or sibling) reminds them of the rule, rather than respond contritely, a response that would likely de-escalate a situation, they are more likely to respond defiantly or with anger. Even if they can repeat the rules and consequences for not following the rules when asked, the pursuit of a rewarding, pleasurable experience interferes with their better judgment.

Helping children understand the rules is only part of the solution for easily frustrated children. The other part of the solution, and perhaps the more relevant part for easily frustrated children, is the consistency of follow-through, which we discuss shortly. In any case, having conversations about why an expectation or rule is in place is useful. It is recommended that these conversations take place when neither the child nor the parent is angry or frustrated so that the child can process and absorb the information. Attempts at reasoning while in the midst of a heated situation are rarely successful. However, following this strategy of reasoning, providing the reasons for the rules or expectations when everyone is calm, doesn't necessarily work very well with easily frustrated children because when they are in a provocative situation they become easily flooded with anger and don't always behave in the way they otherwise know is expected. It's important to note that these children can sometimes then turn their anger on themselves, growing frustrated with themselves for acting the way they did and hurting their relationships or losing privileges.

Research also shows that parents respond to their easily frustrated children with decreases in their consistent limit-setting. Parents may tire of trying to enforce rules over and over in what feels like futile attempts to have an orderly and peaceful household, and they might actually let things their children do slide because they can't bear to have another battle over bedtime or eating vegetables or cleaning a bedroom. Although children who are easily frustrated elicit less consistency from their parents over time, their parents' inconsistent limit-setting practices in turn actually increase children's frustration and anger reactivity. In other words, children's style of frustration and parents' harsh, negative, and inconsistent responses can exacerbate each other over time and can escalate into significant relationship and adjustment problems.

WHAT WORKS BEST WITH EASILY FRUSTRATED CHILDREN?

Children who are highly and easily frustrated can be genuinely challenging to parents and can evoke our worst parenting behaviors. But our interactions with our frustrated children do not have to be negative, and instead of escalating into more negative or coercive interactions we can use our interactions to help our children build some skills for managing their anger.

Build an Accepting, Warm Relationship

Prevention—or, in this case, the best parenting—is the best medicine. The relationship we have with our children, before stressful or adverse experiences occur or before an argument or problem arises, is a preventative measure that minimizes damage and negative outcomes in those situations. Having a relationship in which we demonstrate our unconditional love and affection for our children, in which we communicate to our children that we accept them just the way they are, and that we genuinely enjoy being with them, is the first and most critical step in promoting our children's well-being. This is true for all children, regardless of temperament. However, this has a particularly important role for children who are approach- and reward-oriented. For these children, our warm, accepting, positive relationship is rewarding and something our children will want or gravitate toward, just like other rewarding experiences for them. Although they may react to a restriction or rule or request with anger and frustration because they can't have or do something they want, they will also experience their parents as rewarding and enjoyable. Their desire to be in a good place with their parents and be close with them will help balance their frustration and help modulate or regulate their anger.

Maintaining an accepting and warm relationship works in other ways, too. We described in Chapter 3 the parasympathetic system's role in recovering from arousal, in particular respiratory sinus arrhythmia. In fact, respiratory sinus arrhythmia is a fundamental part of maintaining relationships. Its roots are thought to lie in survival of the species through maintaining social connections. If our emotions are regulated and responsive to social cues, then we are more likely to act adaptively around others. For that reason, having relationships that we experience as providing unconditional love, acceptance, and enjoyment helps support the development of respiratory sinus arrhythmia, which in turn helps us recover from emotional arousal more efficiently. So, our accepting, warm relationships with our children can have a soothing effect on their emotional arousal.

There is yet another benefit of building an accepting, warm relationship with our children: It builds trust. When we are working with our children to learn ways of managing their anger, maybe trying to teach them strategies they can use, they are more likely to feel comfortable and trusting receiving this advice, rather than feeling judged or criticized, because they know you love and accept them for who they are. Think about what it feels like to get advice from someone who you know has your best interest in mind, compared with someone whom you suspect might have other reasons for giving the advice. It's hard to take advice if we feel criticized or judged. This is true for everyone, but for the easily frustrated child, who may have just violated an expectation or rule and may have just yelled at you or said, "You are so mean," recovering from the situation and trying to calm down and pull themselves together will be easier if they also know that, no matter what, you still accept them.

We provide information about practices parents can use to maintain a warm relationship with their children in Chapter 10, including Active Listening, Child-Led Time, and Validation practices.

Be Calm! Don't Engage With Anger

Speaking of managing anger, it is imperative that parents develop their own tools for managing their angry responses to their children. As we said before, easily frustrated children have an unfortunate knack for drawing out negative, irritated, angry, and harsh responses from their parents. Those responses, in turn, exacerbate children's frustration reactivity styles. So, it is particularly important for parents with children who are easily frustrated—and, for that matter, parents who are themselves highly and easily frustrated—to cultivate in ourselves tools for regulating our own emotional reactions, for being able to pause, collect ourselves, and act intentionally and effectively in our interactions with our angry children. The goals are to avoid the escalating negative coercive cycle and instead respond in a way that rides the wave of our children's emotions, calms them, increases their ability to engage in acceptable behaviors and, in the long run, supports our children developing their own self-regulation capacities. In Chapter 9, we provide some practices and tools for building our own emotion regulation. These include Paced Breathing, STOP, Wise Mind, and Parent Time Out practices.

Be Consistent: Predictability Helps

Imagine delivering a speech that you have practiced only once, and right from the start, things start to go wrong. The microphone is too loud, the screen from which you're reading your speech starts to flicker, and the light on you goes dark. You're most likely to lose your place and lose your composure and not be able to deliver the speech. But imagine the same situation delivering a speech that you have rehearsed so many times that you are able to give it from memory. Even though you might be overwhelmed with stress or anxiety with all the things going wrong, you are more likely to be able to get through the speech successfully. You might even be able to smile. Similarly, think about being tested on something that you have barely learned versus something you have memorized, or your ability to effectively handle a near-collision with another car when you first learned to drive versus several years later, when driving skills are second nature. What these all have in common is that our performance on something is better if we can kick into autopilot when something goes wrong or when we are flooded with emotion. In fact, one of the main "active ingredients" of successful parent training programs aimed at enhancing effective parenting is providing opportunities for such rehearsal and practice. This is the reason that parent consistency is so important in children who are easily frustrated. As we discussed in Chapter 4, being consistent refers to having clear, reasonable expectations and rules and consistently reinforcing them so that the privileges in a household are earned when we follow the rules and expectations, and those privileges are lost, or there may be consequences or reparations required, when we don't follow expectations and rules.

For most children, being consistent most of the time is good enough. They get the rules and can usually follow them. However, for children who are highly and easily frustrated, arousal can produce a flood of emotions that make it difficult to remember and follow the rules and expectations. This is not intended to provide them with an excuse and an out for not following family rules. Instead, it helps us understand how they can know and recite back the rules and expectations, seemingly understanding them, and still not always be able to follow through. For easily frustrated children, very consistent follow-through with expectations and rules helps the expected behaviors and the consequences for not following rules become habitual, clear, and inevitable. The more habitual, clear, and inevitable the behaviors and consequences, the more salient they are, even in times of emotional arousal. In other words, consistency will facilitate keeping the expectations, rules, and potential consequences for breaking the rules at the forefront of their attention and help them act on that information even when they are flooded with emotion.

Focus on Positive Reinforcement Rather Than Negative Consequences

A great thing about children who are easily frustrated is that often they are easily frustrated because they are approach- and reward-oriented.

They get more easily and intensely frustrated because they have a stronger drive or motivation to attain their goals, the things that are desirable and pleasurable to them. Although that makes them more likely to experience frustration when they can't have or do what they want, it also gives them a motivation to work toward the things they want. Children who are approach- and reward-oriented are more responsive to working toward something that is reinforcing than they are responsive to negative consequences or punishments. They are more likely to follow a direction or a request if they can earn the privilege of electronics time for doing it rather than losing the privilege for not doing it. With easily frustrated children, parents are more likely to be effective by tuning in to what their children find rewarding or reinforcing and having them work toward a goal of earning those reinforcers by meeting family expectations and rules. See the "Be Consistent: Developing a Behavior Management Plan" worksheet at the end of Chapter 12, which will help you think through some expectations and potential reinforcers for increasing desirable child behaviors.

Remember That All Emotions Are Acceptable, But Not All Behaviors Are

A significant challenge for parents of highly and easily frustrated children is distinguishing getting children in trouble for unacceptable behaviors and not just for being angry, frustrated, or annoying. Earlier, we discussed the importance of accepting and validating children's feelings in a situation, recognizing that any emotional response is a valid response and that validating a feeling is not equivalent to saying that the child's behavior in a situation is acceptable (see Chapter 4). If a child raises her voice to say that something is upsetting her, she is expressing her feelings, and raising one's voice or having a shaky or raspy voice is a natural consequence of being physiologically and emotionally aroused. We don't want to get a child in trouble or have consequences for that. Actually, putting those feelings into words is often a first and important step to getting on top of the feelings. However, if a child raises her voice to say she's angry by leveling insults, criticisms, or curse words at someone, then those are disrespectful and unacceptable behaviors and would warrant the consequence your family uses for unacceptable behaviors. If a child is intensely angry, goes to his room and punches his pillow or bed, he's probably using some pretty effective strategies for relieving some of the physiological arousal and emotional pressure of being angry and would not earn a negative consequence as he would if he instead threw something at someone or damaged a wall or door by hitting it.

Even if this makes sense as you are reading it, in a heated moment when our child is raising his or her voice toward us, we can forget to distinguish appropriate expressions of emotions that can actually de-escalate a situation from inappropriate behaviors. We might be so angry ourselves that we are not thinking clearly, and we experience the child's anger as an affront, reacting with our own inappropriate behaviors, like criticisms, insults, yelling, and piling on consequences or punishments. Our children will learn appropriate ways to express and deal with their anger if we also demonstrate those when we are angry, and we offer some strategies for effectively managing our own emotional reactions in Chapter 9. Overall, when a family has clear, reasonable, and developmentally appropriate expectations and rules about what acceptable and unacceptable behaviors are, and those are consistently upheld and enforced by everyone in the family, easily frustrated children learn over time to manage their anger more effectively. Practices for consistency are presented in Chapters 12 and 13, which also include a reflection on scaffolding versus consequences, the "Be Consistent: Developing a Behavior Management Plan" worksheet, and information about how to use consequences effectively.

When Possible and Appropriate, Help the Child Meet Their Goal

Many frustrated or angry reactions from children will stem from them feeling blocked from attaining a goal. In some of those cases, they are being blocked from something they want, or want to do, that is not allowed. But some of the time, it's not the goal that's not allowed, it's the means by which they are trying to attain the goal. For example, you may walk into your child's room to find her climbing on the furniture. You give the directive to get down from the furniture, and your easily frustrated child's temper flares up, so that she is arguing with you about getting down. It may be that your child's goal in climbing the furniture was to accomplish something unacceptable, like jumping off of the top of the dresser into a pile of stuffed animals you notice on the floor. That might not be allowed in your home because your child could get hurt. On the other hand, your child may be climbing on the furniture because she couldn't reach the tea set that is on the top of the dresser, and she's trying to have a tea party with her stuffies. When a parent walks into this situation, gives a directive to get down, and is met with an angry response from the child, the parent might be less likely to try to understand what the motive or goal behind the action was. If the parent and child engage each other angrily, an opportunity for scaffolding a child's problem solving might be lost.

If, as parents, we are able to maintain our calm in a situation like that, it is useful to pause and listen and try to understand what the child was trying to accomplish. Easily frustrated children might be angry and find it difficult to articulate their goals in those situations. But if parents are able to pause and listen and work to understand the goal, we might learn that the goal was acceptable, but the strategy was not, and we might be able to help our children think through alternative options for attaining their goals. In the example just given, when the child is yelling and arguing that she needs to be climbing the dresser, the parent can clarify why she is climbing the dresser—what is she trying to do? If she was trying to jump into her stuffed animals, then the parent can proceed with her request that the child get off the dresser and follow through with that request. But if the child was trying to get her tea set, the parent can suggest that, given that climbing on the furniture is dangerous and against the rules in this family, there might be alternative ways to reach the tea set, like getting a step stool or asking someone taller to help.

Allowing the child to identify an acceptable alternative can help defuse a situation that otherwise might escalate. Several parenting practices that can support this kind of scaffolding of goals are presented in Chapters 10 and 11 and include Active Listening and Validation practices.

Build Child Anger-Management Tools

Being present, warm, and consistent as a parent will go a long way in helping your child manage his or her frustrated and angry reactions and, in the process, it might also help to convey to your child some strategies they can use for regulating their own emotional arousal. The very best way for parents to teach these strategies to their children is to use them effectively themselves.

The first step is for parents to practice emotion regulation strategies regularly to become more effective at using them. Parents can also articulate that they are trying to use these strategies. Saying so, like a narrator or game announcer, can model for your child when and how to use the strategies and communicates to your child that you are making an effort to interact more effectively with them. This should not be a preachy or "I'm-better-than-you" kind of thing. A parent can just say something like, "I'm pretty angry right now, and I need a minute to take a few breaths and think about how I want to respond to this situation. I don't want to hurt your feelings or make the situation worse, so just give me a minute."

When a parent has been practicing emotion regulation strategies and is getting better at them, they might let the child know that they are working and might invite the child to try them. The wrong time to do this is in a heated situation when either the parent or child is angry. A parent would NOT want to say in a heated moment, "You know, you really need to be doing some of the paced breathing that I've been doing because you have got to get on top of your anger." That would not be effective and will most likely alienate your child to these strategies.

The best time to start sharing these strategies with your child is during a neutral time, in a normal, everyday conversation. A parent might say something like, "I don't know if you've noticed, but when I'm angry, I've been practicing this thing called '+2 Breathing.' It's really pretty easy, and I wanted to show it to you because I think you might want to practice it and try it sometimes when you get frustrated, like doing chores or taking a test at school or something like that." Remember that teaching or coaching a child in these kinds of things always starts with a foundation of an accepting, warm, and predictable relationship. Also, this conversation should take place when things are relatively calm—not in the midst of a disagreement or argument. Scaffolding for regulating anger and frustration more effectively is critical. A child, let alone a parent, will not be able to use these skills easily or immediately. A parent might want to start by setting aside a time to demonstrate and practice together for a couple of minutes in a completely neutral situation. Then the parent and child might spontaneously practice the skill in a fun or playful way, like during pretend play or in the car on the way to the grocery store or when watching TV or a movie and one of the characters starts to get emotional. A parent could say, "Oh, that looks like a time someone could use +2 Breathing. Too bad she doesn't know about it. Let's do two paced breaths for her." If there is a heated situation when either the child or parent gets frustrated or angry, afterward, when everyone is calm, a parent could say, "I think we could have used our STOP strategy [Chapter 9] a few minutes ago. Let's try it now."

Over time, these kinds of practice opportunities will increase the likelihood that your child will use the tools when it counts. Better yet, your child might be learning similar kinds of strategies at school or from the media, and inviting your child to teach you some new emotion regulation or anger management skills will increase your child's confidence in using them and being able to teach you something, too. Children often enjoy the opportunity to be the "expert" and teach parents these kinds of skills.

CONCLUSION

Children who are easily frustrated have strong emotional reactions to being blocked from something they want, and often their reactions are stronger than one would expect in the situation. These children can often react with anger or frustration toward their parents or other adults when they set a limit or enforce a rule. Parents, in turn, more often respond with anger, harsh comments, or punishments. In this chapter, we have suggested some strategies that can be more effective with children who are easily frustrated. Parents can build their own emotion regulation strategies so that they are able to respond calmly and reasonably. It is important to note that using preventive approaches can make a difference. Parents can proactively build their positive relationship with their child, which the child will experience as rewarding, and can encourage and reinforce desired behaviors. Parents can ensure that they have established clear, developmentally appropriate expectations and rules that they consistently enforce, and they can focus on increasing rewards instead of punishments. Parents can also work to understand their children's goals and the sources of their frustration and provide coaching for managing their emotions and developing more effective strategies for meeting these goals. Although for some parents this might seem like a lot of work, the payoff will be less time spent dealing with angry outbursts, arguing over expectations, and more time in positive interactions with your child, allowing you to enjoy their passionate approach to life.

CHAPTER 7

THE IMPULSIVE CHILD

My (Liliana's) son tended to be impulsive, and this showed up mostly in the more structured setting of his classroom or while being coached on a sports team. He was always listening and absorbing information, but it didn't look like it because he would be looking around, watching what others were doing, and sometimes getting up out of his seat in the classroom. However, if he was asked by the teacher or coach to repeat what they said, because they assumed he wasn't listening, he could repeat much of it verbatim. He was also really proud of himself when he knew the answer to a teacher's question, but he often forgot to raise his hand before blurting out the answer and so was frequently reprimanded for not raising his hand. In addition, he found it difficult to stay in his seat when he had something he really wanted to tell his friend across the room, and he didn't plan well enough to pretend to be sharpening his pencil to give him a reason to cross the room, like his friends would do. These are characteristic impulsive behaviors in a classroom or structured setting, and they can be incredibly frustrating to teachers and coaches and disruptive to the group.

These behaviors can also be frustrating to parents when their children break rules or don't do what they are supposed to do at home. A parent might have clearly stated why the child should not run out into the street after a ball, and to always look both ways before crossing a street. But then when the ball rolls out into the street, the child runs right after it without pausing to think about safety. Or an impulsive child might repeatedly ask to play video games right after school, despite the frequently stated rule that they must do their homework before playing video games. Usually the child knows the rule and can repeat both the rule and the reason for it. However, the allure of a desired or rewarding activity overwhelms the child's approach system and often leads to behaviors that might be frustrating for parents.

However, it is also frustrating and demoralizing for the impulsive child who often has a positive intention (e.g., "I'm excited to show the teacher what I know!" or "I can't wait to show my parent my new skill!") but flawed execution (e.g., forgetting to raise their hand or forgetting to look both ways before going into the street). For example, when my (Liliana's) son turned 2, we were celebrating his birthday at a baseball game. The stadium was crowded, and we instructed our children to stay near us and, of course, we held their hands. However, at one point, our son slipped his hand out of mine without trying to tell me what he was doing. He ran about 10 yards away into a crowd. We were calling to him to come back and feeling a little panicked when we lost sight of him. However, then we saw what he was doing. He had seen that a baby in a stroller had dropped his stuffed animal, and his parents hadn't noticed. My son ran over, picked up the stuffie, and handed it to the baby. Excellent intention, poor execution.

In this chapter, we discuss some specific aspects of parent–child interactions when children are more impulsive. We offer some suggestions for an effective approach to managing impulsive behaviors. Of course, it's important to recognize that impulsive behaviors are not always problematic, such as an example we provide later of jumping on an opportunity to drive a boat. Also, in adulthood fast actions can be praised as "decisive," with those taking such actions viewed as leaders. As parents, we can help our more impulsive children find niches where their natural tendencies to act quickly and not worry so much about rules can be valued.

CAUSES AND CONSEQUENCES OF IMPULSIVITY

Impulsive behaviors stem from the behavioral activation system, which contributes to how sensitive a person is to rewards or positive reinforcement (see Chapter 3). It motivates approach behaviors, that is, going after what the person wants. It also motivates active avoidance of negative, threat, or punishment cues. In other words, these children have a hard time making themselves do something they don't want to do. When coupled with low self-regulation or effortful control, an individual who is highly reward oriented has little capacity to inhibit an inappropriate response or slow down to plan how to be more effective or safe. For impulsive children, the reward aspects of a situation outshine the possible consequences, such as the consequence for not finishing a chore or homework, for breaking a family rule, or the risk of doing something unsafe, like running into the street after a ball. The result is that impulsive children often fail to stick with a task or follow directions, and more often they break rules or do risky things.

Impulsive children spend most of their lives hearing things like "What is wrong with you?!" "Are you lazy? Dense? You just don't learn." These children tend to act first and think second. Impulsive children typically struggle with putting the brakes on because of less advanced frontal lobe brain-based regulation, which can change over the course of development as frontal lobe structures mature and gain connectivity. As noted, impulsivity in not just a risk factor when it comes to attention-deficit/hyperactivity disorder: It is actually a symptom of this disorder in its extreme form, that is, when impulsive acts cause distress or impairment and occur in the context of inattention and hyperactivity. Impulsive children may struggle with disruptive behaviors, aggression, and problems with academic achievement when appropriate support from their caregivers and the school is lacking. Impulsivity has been shown to increase risk of injury from accidents, and increase other risky behaviors in adolescence, including alcohol and drug use.

On the other hand, impulsivity can be an asset under certain circumstances and when additional risk factors are absent (i.e., there is no significant inattention, in low-danger situations). Impulsive children can be perceived as decisive, a trait that is often considered an important aspect of leadership, earning respect of their peers and adults alike. They also are more free in enjoying and relishing in the rewarding aspects of their experiences. They can just dive in and have fun.

One time, my (Liliana's) family was in Boston with me for a conference. My kids were 7 years, 4 years, and 7 months old, and my husband took our three kids on a duck boat ride. These are the vehicles that can drive on the road and cruise in the water. Once it was in the water, the tour guide asked the passengers if any of the children wanted to drive the boat. My oldest daughter's (the more fearful one) eyes grew wide, she moved to the edge of her seat, she glanced at the guide and glanced at my husband, visibly giving the offer serious consideration. She asked my husband if she should do it. However, it was already too late. My 4-year-old son, who was reward oriented and viewed this opportunity as too good to miss, was already in the driver's seat steering the boat. He went after the opportunity without pause.

HOW IMPULSIVE CHILDREN RESPOND TO THEIR PARENTS

Children who are impulsive seem to ignore the rules, as if they are breaking the rules on purpose. Sometimes they are engaging in something dangerous or breaking a rule immediately, at the same time that the parent is trying to direct them not to do the thing—that is, the child's reaction is faster than the parent's directions. They can usually repeat back what is expected, and yet they break the rule over and over. For example, when asked by their teacher, "What are you supposed to do before blurting out the answer?" the child can respond, "Raise my hand." Then they usually hear something disparaging, such as "So why don't you?!" or "So what's the problem?!" If you're a parent with a child who tends to be impulsive, you might have heard yourself saying, "How many times have I told you not to . . . ?" Children who are impulsive hear these slights often and in many contexts. They may develop a negative sense of themselves, viewing themselves as "bad," possibly with increasing depression. This might manifest in several ways. Children can grow frustrated and angry, lashing out with oppositional behavior or aggression. They might also withdraw from social situations and struggle to maintain friendships.

HOW PARENTS RESPOND TO IMPULSIVE CHILDREN

Parents of children who are high in impulsivity often experience frustration with their children not following instructions or directions. It feels like their children are not listening to them or willfully disobeying them. A parent can give a direction—for example, not to run across the street—and 5 minutes later that is exactly what the child does. It can feel like parents are talking to a brick wall, as though the child isn't listening or learning from past experiences. Parents can also feel self-conscious about what other people think of them, that they are ineffective in managing their child. My (Masha's) memories of this are still very clear. Being a clinical child psychologist in a small community, I would often see families I have worked with and colleagues in public. When my daughter behaved in particularly challenging ways out shopping, for example, I often felt like all eyes were on me, judging me personally and professionally.

One particularly frustrating thing about children who are impulsive is that, in a neutral situation, they can tell you the rules, expectations, and the consequences for not meeting them. For example, if you ask your impulsive child, "What is the rule about playing by the street?" or "Why do we have a rule about not running into the street?" the child can tell you what the rule is and the reason for it: that it is dangerous because a person can get hit by a car or cause an accident. But the moment that their ball rolls across the street, the child runs across the street without looking both ways. They know the rules and can articulate them. That is not the problem. The problem is that their reward-oriented brain makes it so that the reward of the situation (getting back the ball) is much more salient than the potential threat of danger or negative consequences (being in or causing an accident). As a result, parents can often increase their use of ineffective parenting strategies in a number of ways. Parents sometimes become more harsh, yelling, criticizing, and even using physical punishment out of frustration with their children seemingly not listening to them. Parents also become increasingly inconsistent in response to children's impulsivity. They can feel that their rules, and the consequences for breaking them, are not working, or they might feel tired of their children not meeting those expectations and rules and, as a result, not follow through consistently. Finally, parents might become disengaged, exhausted by repeating the rules and expectations over and over, without apparent impact. All of these parent responses actually lead to increased impulsivity in children.

It is worth mentioning that parents who are easily frustrated might experience more anger toward impulsive children. Also, parents with poor effortful control, who have difficulty with their own attention and emotion regulation, might struggle in maintaining the level of consistency needed to support more optimal development of self-regulation in these children. Both easily frustrated parents and those low in effortful control will benefit from developing the precise direction and reinforcement plan we present in Chapter 12, practicing their approach ahead of implementation. Having a road map for approaching exchanges with an impulsive child wherein risk for power struggles is significant can help parents maintain a reflective stance rather than getting pulled into a heated exchange. In Chapter 9, which focuses on mindful parenting practices, we go into greater detail on this reflective stance, which can support caregivers' own self-regulation, building positive parent–child relationships, and being consistent. Of course, sometimes parents require consultation with a mental health provider, in particular one who specializes in parenting and parent–child relationship issues.

WHAT WORKS BEST WITH IMPULSIVE CHILDREN

To avoid the pitfall of risky trajectories marked by conduct and school problems, impulsive children require firm, basic directions from their caregivers with support, guidance, and structuring. This might require a shift in perspective from viewing your child as willfully breaking the rules or not listening to recognizing that they need help in solving a particular challenge. Children who are impulsive require structure and scaffolding to increase their opportunities for success and to build their self-regulation capacity. It helps to use brief, clear directions and provide concrete reminders, cues, or tools to support them. In my (Masha's) clinical work, I find that coaching parents to rely on precise directions described in the sections that follow (and in detail in Chapter 12) is extremely effective. Precise directions work because they provide an effective framework for providing firm boundaries and limitations, creating the structure impulsive children require to succeed in meeting adults' expectations.

The suggestions we provide in this chapter are likely to help, but if they don't, do not hesitate to consult with your pediatrician or a child mental health provider, who can offer more targeted and individualized recommendations.

Be Calm and Compassionate

Children who are impulsive can try our patience. As parents, we can become frustrated and tired of the constant need for structure and reminders. Parents often resort to yelling or increasingly harsh comments or punishments or, conversely, can become distant and disengage from trying to support their child. Both of these responses will likely have the effect of increasing the child's impulsivity. Parents can practice being calm and present using some of the mindfulness and emotion regulation practices that we present in Chapter 9. Practicing mindfulness for a few minutes every day can increase parents' capacity to remain calm and present in challenging or emotionally charged situations.

Wise Mind (see Chapter 9) is also a useful practice in engaging with impulsive children. In Wise Mind, we are mindful of both our emotions and our thoughts in a situation. We hold and observe these in the moment, recognizing both are present and valid. We then work to find a balanced or middle way between our emotions and thoughts. We ask ourselves, "What is needed? What will be effective?" This might mean letting go of being "right" in a situation, seeing the situation from your child's perspective, tuning into how your child is feeling, and focusing on how to be effective in supporting your child meeting the expectation or rule.

Be Warm and Rewarding

Warm, supportive relationships will be experienced as rewarding to these reward-oriented children. Engage them in activities they view as fun, and if these provide opportunities for conversation you may be able to impart some wisdom along with enjoying each other's company. They will be more engaged and less likely to tune out your guidance and directives. If the parent–child relationship becomes conflictual, impulsive children will actively avoid interactions with parents, tuning them out when they try to provide guidance. When the child has a strong, positive relationship with a parent, maintaining that relationship as a rewarding and fulfilling part of their life facilitates their commitment to working on meeting expectations.

Provide Guidance at the Right Times

In general, impulsive children are not amenable to lectures, because lectures are boring. Guidance is best delivered via streamlined and carefully placed content, provided in a positive or neutral tone, not a negative critical one, which will be immediately disregarded. Ideally, mindful parents drop guidance gems spontaneously on unexpecting impulsive children when the opportunity presents itself. For example, when watching a movie or hearing a story about another child making rapid and poorly thought-through choices, a parent can reflect on the fact that this was not an optimal approach, maybe even engaging in a conversation about how better decisions could have been developed and executed (e.g., by talking to adults, or at least thinking through consequences before acting). I (Masha) was recently enjoying bingeing on Stranger Things with my daughter and had many opportunities to reflect on the young characters' impulsive acts, like taking on Russian agents without any adults knowing what they were up to or helping. I found myself saying things like, "OK, if something like this really did happen, would you think about telling your parents or another adult who could help?" This, of course, will not prevent all hasty decision making, but it does create a positive platform from which to have conversations about making good choices and slowing down to figure these out.

It's also useful to revisit situations in which impulsive actions were taken to consider more optimal strategies and lessons learned. The goal is to work together with your child to plan for the next time a similar situation arises and to collaborate on ideas that will set your child up for success before the situation comes up next time. Here is another Masha example. Last winter, I took my daughter skiing with a friend and her daughter, which we have done before but in a larger group and a different location. After going down some easier slopes, my daughter's friend made the decision (and my daughter went along with it) to go it alone, separating from me and my friend who were "too slow," because they did not want to wait for us. After we (the adults) finished a couple of runs, we headed down to the lodge for a break and immediately received a frantic phone call from one of our children: "We don't know where we are . . . there are black diamonds everywhere . . . help!" Well, of course, it was not so easy for us to help, because we didn't know where they were, either. My friend was able to stay calm and talked her daughter through a couple of key choices, and soon we heard that they were skiing towards us. Apparently, shortly after the previous panicked phone call they spotted a toddler followed by his family and were able to follow them to return to the other side of the mountain. By the way, I was definitely not calm—I was imagining a number of terrible possibilities, and I was glad one of us could keep their cool. One of my favorite take-home messages of this experience, and there are many, is how much our daughters underestimated the role of adult guidance in prior skiing adventures—one of the adults always picked the runs. Every now and again, I'll remind my daughter about this experience and say something like: "This seems like something you should plan a bit, so that it's not like that one time. . . ." She does not love these reminders, but they work—she definitely knows what I am talking about.

A note of caution is warranted insofar as such reminders should be provided with care. For example, if your child is already struggling to manage strong emotions, these are not advisable. It is also important to bring up prior incidents with a positive tone, rather than a punitive or controlling one, in a "Let's plan ahead" and "Recall lessons learned" manner rather than "You'll end up making that mistake again" and "You never get things right" spirit. Remember, lectures don't work. These are opportunities to have a conversation, letting your child generate strategies that might work for them. These kinds of reminders and recollections are meant to be tools for setting your child up for success, considering potential options and choices ahead of an event that is likely to challenge a child high in impulsivity.

Provide Scaffolding

Scaffolding is described in detail in Chapter 11. In brief, this means stepping in with guidance and structuring to ensure that the child has the tools and support to successfully complete a task or solve a problem while also providing enough autonomy and independence for them to build the skills on their own. We want to provide enough support for our children to succeed much of the time, but not so much support that they aren't learning anything because we are doing it all for them. Research conducted by Liliana and her colleagues shows that impulsive children who are not given enough structure, guidance, and boundaries only increase in their impulsivity and behavior problems over time (Shimomaeda et al., 2023). This is likely because they end up having more failure experiences than nonimpulsive children and receive criticism from adults and peers around them.

The idea of goodness-of-fit is relevant to this discussion insofar as the level of control exerted by parents should match the needs of the child. Impulsive children inherently require support and structure in meeting expectations, firm boundaries, and consistently enforced limits. They just do not realize it themselves, and they will never thank you for enforcing rules and sticking to consequences. As children gain self-regulation skills and improve in their ability to inhibit maladaptive responses and follow through on activities they do not find enjoyable (e.g., boring homework assignments or chores), parents can pull back on the structure they provide in supporting these behaviors. However, consistent limit-setting is critical to supporting the development of self-regulation, in effect lowering impulsivity, and thus should be maintained as a cornerstone of approaching impulsive children.

Of course, there is a time for more in-depth discussions and explanations regarding why things have to be done a certain way, such as why doing homework right after getting home from school and having a quick snack is better than watching TV or having screen time first. By the way, everyone—in particular, impulsive children who are so reward oriented—finds it much easier to switch from a less pleasant activity to a more pleasant activity (i.e., homework to screen time, or work to vacation) than vice versa. Lectures, lengthy discussions, and explanations are absolutely to be avoided in the moment of attempting to get cooperation from your impulsive child when the goal is to get them to do something they are not inherently interested in doing. Praise is a reward to your child and can be useful in increasing desired behaviors when offered appropriately: immediately, frequently, with enthusiasm, when eye contact is established, describing the desired behavior in some detail, and with variety—don't say the same thing over and over again, it will be repetitive and will not come across as genuine. A good rule of thumb is to offer four praises for every correction or reprimand.

It is best to prepare the child when this approach is coming if previously the expectations regarding cooperation were low and the child was basically allowed to do things the way they wanted, when they wanted. It should not be a mystery that parents are altering their approach to behavior management, and once this family discussion has taken place parents have to follow through on implementation in a consistent manner. Because consistency is so critical for impulsive children, if plans for rewards or negative consequences are introduced, repeated follow-through is essential. As noted, rewards can be more effective when you mix it up. So, you can develop a daily and weekly rewards menu, and have your child pick from it, with a rule of not being able to pick the same thing more than twice in a row. The daily menu should include only things that are really feasible on a daily basis, such as picking a snack, helping to prepare a meal (I have been surprised by how much children enjoy doing this), screen time, an outing to a park or playground, or a family game.

Children who are impulsive also benefit from scaffolding in the form of tools, cues, or prompts to support expected behaviors. For example, a checklist of things that need to get done when the child is supposed to clean their room or complete chores, or a sign on the mirror that lists morning routines, helps cue the expected behaviors. The child can tape a symbol on their desk at school that will remind them to raise their hand. It is important, however, that these aren't so obvious that they embarrass or shame the child. The best approach is to work together to make checklists, signs, and cues. Cocreate and write a schedule for completing homework each day, and make sure that the schedule builds in breaks. It is helpful to break up tasks or expectations into their steps or component parts. It can also be helpful to use code words for slowing or stopping so the child isn't constantly hearing "Stop" or "No." When my (Liliana's) son was young, we would say "Freeze" or "Whoa" instead of saying "Stop" all the time. These were experienced as less aversive, but they carried the same meaning. Key to supporting children who are impulsive is to use a coaching and collaborative approach.

Be Consistent

Consistency in expectations, structure, rewards, and consequences is critical. First, it is critical that our directions and directives to our children are precise and crystal clear, with no room left for misinterpretation. In Chapter 12, we describe using precise directions as an approach to communicating rules and expectations with children. In addition, being consistent in communicating and enforcing expectations or rules is critical. It makes the expectations and consequences more salient, when they are not naturally salient for an impulsive child, at least not more salient than whatever rewarding experience they are pursuing. Think of trying to look at the stars during the day. You can't see them because the sun is too bright. We know the stars are there, but they are invisible in daylight. For a reward-oriented child, the potential consequences for a behavior are not visible because of the brightness of the potential rewarding thing they are going after. Consistency is much more critical with impulsive children than with others to ensure that the consequences for risky or unacceptable behaviors are more salient or visible. They become more ingrained and habitual through repetition and learning.

We should also note that a random or inconsistent schedule of reinforcement or consequences actually increases impulsive behavior. It is similar to gambling: You keep trying because sometimes it pays off. Impulsive children are particularly susceptible to this. Keep in mind that rewards consume a HUGE amount of their attention, whereas negative consequences are tiny hints in the back of their mind. Negative consequences are still important and, to be at the forefront of their attention when making choices, they need to be consistent and meaningful and in line with transgressions: mild consequences for minor transgressions and more significant ones when the rule-breaking or lack of cooperation is more substantial in terms of its impact. We offer suggestions for being consistent in Chapter 12.

Remember to acknowledge, celebrate, and reinforce your children's wins and successes. We are often a lot better at catching their missteps than catching them doing well. Reinforcement comes in a lot of forms, but one of the most potent for children is our time and attention. (See our discussion about practicing "time in" in Chapter 12.) We can also build in rewards for when our children meet expectations. These do not have to be material things or food. A criticism of using positive and negative consequences is that we are treating our children like pets that we are training. This perspective of reinforcement is unfortunate. Keep in mind that there are rewards and negative consequences for everything we do in life. As adults, we are more likely to get a promotion or a raise at work if we do a great job and meet or exceed expectations. If we fail to meet expectations, we might not get promoted, and we might even lose our job. If we leave household maintenance tasks undone for too long, there will often be a more complicated and expensive repair than if we had stayed on top of the maintenance. These are examples of positive and negative consequences of our behaviors that we encounter every day.

With this idea in mind, parents can consider what the natural or fitting positive and negative consequences for their children's behaviors can be. Finishing homework in a timely manner can be rewarded with extra play time. Playing video games or using other electronic devices can be contingent on completing homework or chores around the house. With impulsive children, given that they are reward oriented, building in positive consequences or rewards for meeting expectations is the most effective way to build their commitment to meeting expectations and their capacities for self-regulation. We provide examples of tools for planning rewards and consequences in Chapter 12.

Consistency is critical to parental responses to child impulsive behaviors. If you make a decision to alter the manner in which you manage high levels of impulsivity, perhaps by following some of the guidance given in this chapter, it will be important to follow the new routine as much as possible. Remember, consistency means your child gets more chances to learn from your encouragement and limit-setting, and if you are using a new approach only occasionally then it will not be clear to your child that this is important. Of course, no one can act exactly the same way in different situations across time, or even follow the same general approach in every appropriate instance. However, if you are using a new rewards system, for example, on a daily basis and one day while visiting relatives or friends you are not able to do so, you will be able to explain this deviation from the routine and why this unusual course of action is necessary. You can also remind your child that everyone will be back to the regular routine once you return home.

CONCLUSION

Because impulsivity stems from a sensitivity to rewards coupled with little ability to slow down or refrain from undesirable behaviors, impulsive children often go after something they want without pausing to think or be effective. In addition, they often avoid things or have a hard time making themselves do things that are boring, tedious, or not rewarding. They often forget to finish a task or have a hard time finishing their homework, and they more often break rules or do risky things. These behaviors can be incredibly frustrating for parents and other adults in the impulsive child's life. However, we hope that, in understanding the biological roots of this behavior, parents can see that these behaviors are usually not malicious, and impulsive children are usually not intentionally trying to violate expectations. Parents who are able to build strong, positive relationships; provide guidance and structuring; and be consistent in setting limits may be able to support the development of better self-regulation and reduce children's risk for other problems developing later. When parents and children can settle into routines that strengthen a positive relationship and support children in meeting expectations and following rules, both parents and children can spend more time enjoying children's passions, creating fun and rewarding times together.

CHAPTER 8

THE INFLEXIBLE CHILD

From a very young age, my (Liliana's) youngest showed signs of being somewhat inflexible. In some ways, she was very easygoing—going along with the family on outings, going with the flow of our busy family schedules, and wanting to do whatever her two older siblings were doing. However, in other ways there were things she handled inflexibly. She would insist on changing her clothes if she got a drop of water on her shirt or if there was a small string hanging from her skirt. She would get really upset if she were not able to change, for example, if we were out of the house. She also liked to line up her My Little Ponies in a particular order based on the color and social relationships of the ponies. If her dad moved the ponies around when they were playing, suggesting that Pinkie Pie might want to play with Wisteria for a change, she would grow frustrated and tearful about the disruption. Finally, she struggled to make choices when offered a dessert or an option of something to play. She often asked her siblings or us to choose for her so she wouldn't have to. These were signs of a tendency to be inflexible.

The temperament characteristic of *flexibility* refers to how easily one copes with or adapts to uncertainty and change, or how easily one can shift from doing one thing to another, or to switch gears when solving a problem and the first solution isn't working. The child who is higher in flexibility is more adaptable to change or ambiguity. Conversely, the child who is low in flexibility struggles with change or ambiguity. Sometimes, switching from one task to another or making choices can be a struggle and can create arguments. The child might also get stuck with trying one solution to a problem over and over and grow frustrated and distressed when it isn't working. Often, inflexible children will rely on a go-to choice or option when faced with having to make a choice to avoid uncertainty. For example, the child might order the same thing every time at restaurants to avoid having to make a choice or the uncertainty of what they will get. This characteristic can make children vulnerable to developing anxiety, depression, or behavior problems, and sometimes compulsive behaviors, particularly when they experience a relationship with their parents that is low in warmth and support.

In this chapter, we share approaches shown to be effective with highly inflexible children. Overall, these can be described as gently steering an inflexible child toward greater flexibility, with positive guidance and appropriate expectations, because these need to be age appropriate and because we often measure progress in "baby steps." Regardless of whether a child is inflexible because they are high in fearfulness and avoidance, or they find choices and conflict challenging because of low effortful control abilities, inflexible children need support from adults to make gains in being able to shift gears, make choices in uncertain situations, or adapt to changes. They also need to know that parents expect them to make these gains and believe they can be successful in becoming more flexible.

CAUSES AND CONSEQUENCES OF INFLEXIBILITY

Although we know less about this temperament characteristic from research compared with the dimensions described thus far, it is evident that sensitivity to the environment, anxiety, and inflexible cognitive processes play a role. As noted in Chapter 3, there are two primary pathways that likely contribute to inflexible temperaments: (1) a fear and avoidance pathway, which we have been calling the *behavioral inhibition system (BIS) tendency*, and (2) an executive function or attention-regulation pathway, that is, a less advanced ability to select among alternative options. This results in difficulty with conflict resolution and, ultimately, an avoidance of making choices, both of which are associated with effortful control capacities. However, the fear/avoidance pathway is ultimately subject to attention-based regulation. In other words, for BIS-driven children motivated to avoid novelty and keep everything exactly the same, inflexibility is essentially a coping strategy. More advanced regulation and being able to intentionally focus attention enable an individual to resolve conflicts between options or choices, facilitating effective and flexible decision making. These abilities support a more adaptive coping approach. It follows that being better regulated would be protective in this context, so that even highly fearful or avoidant children could develop strategies that do not create problems of their own, like inflexibility.

Inflexibility can present in a few different ways, and it is sometimes very specific, for example, in organizing toys during play, and sometimes it shows up more broadly. Inflexible children struggle with adaptation to a change in the routine or deviation from their expectations and predictable activities. Most of these behaviors are aimed at achieving predictability: "If I make sure things stay exactly the same and everything in my life is completely predictable, I don't have to experience those unpleasant and uncomfortable feelings." Of course, this is not a conscious or voluntary decision—instead, this temperament style becomes dominant simply because of largely unconscious emotional and learning processes at work. Children understand that they do not like feeling a disruption in their environment and learn that maintaining a rigid behavioral stance ensures they do not have to. As described earlier, this is self-reinforcing. Avoiding the negative feeling by ensuring that nothing is out of place reinforces the behavior of ensuring that nothing is out of place. In addition, children who struggle to resolve a conflict between different available choices would rather avoid having to make a choice, which they do not have to do when everything in their daily life happens in exactly the same manner.

When these behaviors are accommodated, they can become entrenched or extreme. Inflexible children often have significant tantrums and meltdowns when something that they did not anticipate takes place (e.g., a field trip instead of the regular class schedule, going on vacation or being away from home, a substitute teacher who wants to do things differently). Less flexible children also can struggle in their sibling or peer relationships when they are less able to go along with what other children want to play or do. At the extreme, this type of inflexibility may become disruptive to a child's and family's life. This can lead to obsessive-compulsive problems that can interfere with typical day-to-day activities. This level of inflexibility is also sometimes seen in children with an autism spectrum disorder, along with social, communication, or language problems and unusual behaviors.

Although related to a fearful temperament, inflexibility (or coping by ensuring sameness) is ultimately a function of limited self-regulation supported by advanced attentional skills, which are based in the frontal lobes of the brain and benefit from the maturation of those lobes. In this chapter, we explore how inflexibility plays out in parent–child interactions, providing recommendations for addressing these challenges. We offer several parenting strategies aimed at supporting children who tend to be inflexible to build skills for adaptability and resilience.

HOW INFLEXIBLE CHILDREN RESPOND TO THEIR PARENTS

Inflexible children can be pleasant and easygoing as long as their preferred activity is available or regular routine is being followed. So, if they are never challenged with the unpredictable or unanticipated, there may not be any parenting challenges. Responses to parents quickly become unpleasant when changes in routine are introduced, especially if something a child is not comfortable with is substituted for a preferred activity. Of course, new experiences and changes in routine are a part of growing up and generally cannot be avoided. As such, inflexible children often respond to their parents with resistance, which can be accompanied by crying, whining, yelling, defiance, and aggression. Inflexible children often resort to tantrums, which can be severe and long lasting, in an effort to keep things in their comfort zones.

Sometimes, parents are puzzled by changes in child attitude and demeanor and do not understand how an otherwise-pleasant and well-behaved child can turn into a defiant, tantrum-ing one. Upon careful analysis of situations that result in tantrums, crying, whining, and so on, it is often apparent that the reactions of resistance were occurring because of challenges requiring some flexibility in the face of unpredictable or unanticipated events.

HOW PARENTS RESPOND TO INFLEXIBLE CHILDREN

Inflexible children are often perceived as difficult by parents and teachers as well as peers. Parents are impacted whenever the home routine has to be adjusted, which in most families is commonplace. Households that are more chaotic are going to be even more challenging for an inflexible child, who will likely be irritable and may have significant emotional meltdowns because of frequent inconsistencies or shifts in daily routine. Parents will often defer to the rigid structure a child who is inflexible insists on, usually out of frustration or exhaustion with the struggle that ensues when they try to change things. However, other adults, siblings, and peers are usually not as accommodating, and relationships can be strained. Teachers have struggles similar to parents', although more structured classrooms provide a more predictable environment, and in many ways are a better fit for these children. Peer interactions are typically most impacted because same-age children, especially young children, are not as able or willing to accommodate an inflexible play partner or classmate. Not surprisingly, play interactions of young inflexible children often lead to disagreements and meltdowns, whereas older inflexible children may struggle to find stable and supportive relationships.

This is where a parent's own temperament might come into play. Parents who are themselves inflexible might need to recognize this in themselves. Their own tendency toward inflexibility might model inflexibility to their children and, even more, render a parent more likely to accommodate their child's inflexibility, thus reinforcing it. Conversely, parents can serve as models of flexibility, highlighting an example of when a flexible decision was made and worked out. I (Masha) have frequently said to my daughter things like "You know, even though it wasn't my top choice, it ended up being OK getting food at the restaurant Dad wanted." Modeling flexibility is helpful, and it would be difficult to teach flexibility to a child if parents insist on rigidity, because it quickly becomes a "Do as I say, not as I do" situation.

In addition, easily frustrated parents might grow impatient with their children, reacting with frustration or anger, taking a punitive stance or saying critical, hurtful things. Parents can increase their awareness of how their own temperament is interacting with their children's temperament by pausing during challenging situations, using calming Be Present practices, and checking their Wise Mind, which we describe in Chapter 9.

WHAT WORKS BEST WITH INFLEXIBLE CHILDREN?

It is important to note that clinical research and practice offer clear steps to helping children build some flexibility to help support adjustment across contexts. There is an important caveat to the advice that follows: Parents have to be careful to pick their battles. We have to be honest with ourselves about our capabilities and resources in the moment. Do not go down the road of creating challenges to your child's inflexibility, or setting limits, if you are not going to be able to follow through in a matter of fact, clear-headed way with prepared responses to create the structure. If you are not able to do this—and sometimes we are not, because it has been a long day or we faced difficulties at work—do not engage in a power struggle that can turn into something damaging to the relationship with your child (e.g., you saying things that you do not really want to say). Avoid unnecessary power struggles and give in early when you have a sense that the timing for challenging your child's inflexibility is not right for whatever reason. Be prepared by practicing the Be Present skills offered in Chapter 9. Also, have a clear plan for Being Consistent, such as the one we present in Chapter 12.

Balance Validation and Structure

As noted in Chapter 2, inflexible children struggle with adaptation to any change in the routine or deviation from their expectations and predictable activities, or in situations that are uncertain. It is typical to hear them complain that something "doesn't feel right," especially when they are younger and understandably having a hard time articulating the nature of their experience. Parents of inflexible children have the challenge of striking a balance between showing empathy with respect to this experience while at the same time creating structure designed to encourage flexibility. Let's tackle the empathy part first.

An important part of being empathic is trying to sort out whether you are dealing with inflexibility that is primarily rooted in fear/anxiety or a conflict-resolution (executive function) pathway. For a child who is in fact highly fearful and copes with this predisposition by adapting a rigid approach—"If I make sure things stay exactly the same, and everything in my life is completely predictable, I don't have to experience those unpleasant and uncomfortable feelings"—it will be important to understand the nature of the primary fears involved. It is often useful to develop some hypotheticals aimed at discerning the worst-case scenario: "What is the worst thing that can happen, the worst thing you are afraid of happening?" You will often find out that either the worst thing is not really that bad, or it is highly unlikely. The "not that bad" case is pretty straightforward—you talk about the fact that this would not actually be terrible, that the child could cope with this situation in a reasonable, adaptive manner. For the "not very likely, but not impossible" scenario it will be important to have discussions regarding the difference between possibility and probability. In other words, something might be possible, but also very unlikely to happen, so that preparing for it and worrying about what to do if it happens, is just not practical. Sure, even a home located on a hill and completely land locked could experience a flood, but this misfortune is much more likely to strike low-lying properties and those next to bodies of water.

Another important theme to develop with a child for whom something "doesn't feel right" is that *uncomfortable* doesn't mean *dangerous*. So, for example, putting socks on when the weather gets cold in the fall might feel uncomfortable after the barefoot, sandal-and-flip-flop summer, but socks are not going to hurt your feet—at least, there has never been a reported case of hurt feet because of wearing socks. Everyone has to do some things that might feel uncomfortable—give examples from your own life when you've had to go out on a limb and do things that felt uncomfortable or scary. I (Masha) like to tell the story of being in my yoga class and working on my handstand. It felt uncomfortable and scary, particularly because I was trying to go up next to a window, and I was starting to have thoughts of crashing through the glass. This is when it dawned on me that I was experiencing anxiety, that the likelihood of crashing through the window was minimal, and my discomfort was not a sign of actual danger, just a cue related to the novelty of the situation. One more comment about being empathic: These are not conversations to be had when you are trying to insist on boundaries or are already in the midst of a power struggle. If the latter is happening, use Precise Directions (Chapter 12), and have a more in-depth conversation later wherein you are responsive and empathic.

To successfully increase a child's flexible approach to things, a parent needs to balance validation and structure. By validating how a child feels, parents let their children know that their feelings are real and understandable. That does not mean that their feelings accurately reflect the risk in the situation of deviating from a routine but rather that the parents understand the sources of their children's feelings. We offer guidance for validation in Chapter 10. "Providing structure" refers to slowly and gently encouraging deviations from the routines that provide comfort. Next, we offer suggestions for doing this with successive approximations.

Provide Scaffolding and Successive Approximations

In Chapter 11, we present the parenting practice of *Scaffolding*—knowing when to step in with guidance and structuring and when to step back and allow your child the autonomy to make their own choices. Using the concept of scaffolding as a guide, parents can create small, intentional challenges to the inflexible behavior. For example, with my (Liliana's) daughter, mentioned at the start of this chapter, if she got a drop of water on her shirt or had a string hanging from a piece of clothing, I would ask her to wait for a bit before changing, setting a timer and slowly increasing the amount of time. She started with 1 minute, then 2 minutes, and eventually increasing to 5 minutes. I encouraged her to go back to playing while she waited, or I distracted her with a fun activity. This showed her that she could actually tolerate the discomfort of the problem with her clothing and nothing terrible would happen. It also showed her that the drop of water would quickly dry, and that the string could be trimmed without the need to change her clothes. These small, successive challenges build up the child's distress tolerance while also showing the child that the dreaded outcome does not usually come to pass. These small, increasing challenges can be thought of as *successive approximations* of the ultimately desired behavior. They can be used to encourage a child to play a little differently with their favorite toys, or to follow a slightly different routine when getting ready to go out, with successive iterations gently challenging the child to try to tolerate something a little different, or a little longer.

Another strategy parents can use effectively involves getting things wrong on purpose, but in a way that it appears they have not done it on purpose. We know, this sounds manipulative. However, it will help your inflexible child become more flexible, so it is worth it in the long run. Here are some examples to illustrate this approach. You have a child who insists on always eating chicken nuggets when you go to McDonald's, and you would like them to expand their food repertoire. You could get takeout and come home with a cheeseburger instead, informing your son or daughter, "They were all out of chicken nuggets. . . .We tried to get them for you but could not." If your child is very reluctant to eat the cheeseburger, tell them to just take a few bites—this opens the door to trying different foods. You will need to do this more than once, but if you stick to creating similar situations you will be nudging your child toward flexibility. If you have a child who is super-sensitive to the texture of clothing and does not like the new shirt you got because "it doesn't feel right," you can tell them, "I am right in the middle of something, please keep it on for 10 minutes then we can talk about it." Again, this approach does not get you out of this struggle completely, but it does encourage your child to show more flexibility. One more example: Your inflexible child wants to have the same book read at bedtime every night, no exceptions. You can have the book disappear for an evening and tell them something like, "We let the neighbors borrow that book, just for tonight. Their son/daughter is sick and they really needed something to cheer him/her up." Encourage your child to pick a different book. If they have trouble choosing, you pick two books that you say you would really like to read, and have your child pick one.

Use Wise Mind and Structuring Choices

For the child who struggles with making choices, you have to provide more practice with making choices—yes, exactly the thing that they do not wish to do. Make decision-making part of the daily routine: choosing outfits, breakfast, snacks, family games, movies, and so on. The only rule is that any of the choices you offer have to be acceptable if chosen—that is, if everyone is going to be watching TV together that evening, do not offer a movie that would not be appropriate for your entire family to watch. You can also explain to your child that not making a decision in fact constitutes making a choice, and probably the least preferred one, but again, not in the midst of setting limits or dealing with a power struggle. Again, Precise Directions, discussed in Chapter 12, can be very helpful in these instances. You also have to be thoughtful about how choices are presented, so if you are going to offer different outfits for school it would be best to do this the night before, in case the inflexible child is struggling, ensuring there is plenty of time for decision making and any recovery from distress that likely will happen. It can also help to make the choices as simple as possible and start by offering two choices or allowing the child to narrow a wider range of choices down to two and then say that you'll make the final choice. Over time, slowly increase the number of choices, or switch roles and have your child make the final choice after you've narrowed it down.

It also helps to start by practicing choices that have low stakes and low stress. If choosing a meal at a restaurant or picking an outfit for the day creates distress, those might not be the best things to start practicing. Instead, choosing between two cookie options for dessert, or between two different color socks, might be easier places to start. If your child has a go-to answer or option, they might be offered a choice between two alternative things. If your child always chooses Oreo cookies, maybe offer them the choice between oatmeal and chocolate chip, to change things up a little. Of course, what is high or low stakes will be different for each child, so it will be helpful if you assess which situations cause more or less stress.

Be Present and Flexible

Regardless of the primary pathway, the end result is the same: Inflexible children can have significant tantrums and meltdowns when something that they did not anticipate takes place. As parents, we can help them adjust to unanticipated events by using the approaches outlined in this chapter. We also have to model flexibility ourselves, demonstrating adjustment in the face of change and coping with shifting demands we encounter.

One additional note: The advice presented in this chapter is for typically developing children with challenging temperament profiles resulting in limited flexibility. If your child is experiencing obsessive or compulsive behaviors that interfere with their quality of life, your family might benefit from seeking support from a therapist. In addition, if you suspect that your very inflexible child may be on the autism spectrum, please seek a professional consultation and evaluation.

CONCLUSION

Children who tend to be inflexible most likely have an underlying BIS-driven temperament, coupled with a less advanced ability to select among alternative options, which is a component of effortful control.

Although a less advanced capacity for self-regulation is a critical part of inflexibility because it limits children's ability to turn to a different and more adaptive (albeit less practiced) strategy, understanding the contribution of fearfulness and avoidance is important. For children who rely on inflexibility to cope with fearfulness, parents need to understand the nature of fear and avoidance to be most helpful and effective in managing this trait. These children also benefit from reminders that feeling uncomfortable or awkward is not the same as something being dangerous and that they can learn to tolerate some uncomfortable feelings.

Overall, what constitutes an effective response for children who struggle with choices is giving them opportunities to make these in small doses. These opportunities should be predictable (e.g., introduced in advance, consistently presented) with ample time to manage decision making, for example, leaving plenty of time in the evening to make decisions regarding the school lunch or outfit for the next day. Learning to be more flexible does not have to be tedious if the choices are all acceptable, for example, when all lunch options are your child's preferred foods and the unselected ones can be enjoyed later. Sometimes, making sure that there is one clear front-runner (one favorite outfit among presented options) will help you and your child, and making good choices can be rewarded. Having a positive and supportive relationship with your child overall is also important to mention because this foundation needs to come first. Do things together—enjoy activities with your child, talk about things you both enjoy, plan fun activities. These are all important in their own right and will help you in building your child's flexibility.

III

THE CORE PARENTING PRINCIPLES

CHAPTER 9

BE PRESENT

In this chapter, we describe practices that support parents to be present in the moment; to notice and observe without making assumptions or judgments; and to be calm and effective, bringing our best selves to our interactions with our children. Some of these are mindfulness practices we can do anywhere and anytime, and some we can use in our relationships and interactions with our children.

+2 BREATHING

+2 Breathing is an exercise that you can do in just a few minutes anytime and anywhere. It is a great way to collect yourself after a crazy day, or a way to help you get back to the present moment when you can't get your mind off of something that happened in the past or stop worrying about something that may happen in the future. These skills are a great way to prepare yourself for interacting with your child in the most positive and effective way possible every time—it's hard to be effective if our minds are somewhere else or if we are emotionally upset. +2 Breathing is a great way to collect ourselves, bring ourselves to be present, and calm ourselves if we are feeling emotional or stressed.

+2 Breathing is when we breathe out a little longer than we breathe in. When we breathe in, our heart speeds up and we get energized to focus and act. When we breathe out, our heart slows down and our body calms down. So, if we take a deep long breath in, and then make our breath out a little longer than our breath in, we can gain energy and focus and then slow down our heart rate, calm down, and become more focused. Let's try this. Visit https://ccfwb.uw.edu/resource/2-breathing-2/ to hear an audio recording of someone guiding you through the practice. Here's what you do:

- Get your body in an awake and holdable position. Let's start by sitting up straight and opening up our shoulders and chest. This makes it easier to breathe deeply. Have your eyes looking downward and softly focused on something in the room, such as something on the floor a few feet in front of you.
- Our second step is noticing our breath.
- Breathe in and out at a normal pace. Notice your breath. Notice breathing in and out. Do this for two or three breaths.
- With your next breath, practice taking a *diaphragmatic*, or "belly" breath. Take your hand and place it just below your sternum, right at the top of your stomach. That's about where your diaphragm is. Place your other hand on your chest. When you breathe in, feel your diaphragm expanding. Your chest should not expand much. Instead, when you really take air deep into your lungs, your diaphragm or belly should expand like a balloon. Your lower hand should move more than your upper hand. So, for your next two or three breaths, take deep diaphragm breaths.
- Next, count how many seconds your inhale, your breath in, is when you take a deep diaphragm breath. Do this for two or three breaths.
- Now, as you breathe out, add 2 seconds to your breath out. Make your exhale a little longer than your inhale. Try this for your next two or three breaths.

- Breathe in, and count. Then breathe out and count 2 more seconds.
- Your mind may wander to other things. If it does, notice this, gently bring it back to breathing and counting for two or three more breaths.
- Breathe in and then breathe out 2 seconds longer. You don't have to keep counting, but sometimes that can help anchor your attention when your mind is racing or ruminating.
- Breathe in and out like this two more times.

What did you notice during the exercise? How did that feel? Is there something about it that was hard or didn't seem right? Is there something that you're concerned about in doing it?

Once or twice a day, try to practice +2 Breathing. It only takes a couple of minutes. Do it when you have a couple of quiet minutes, like before getting dressed or just after getting up, or while taking a short break at work. It might help to tape a card or sticky note to your mirror or refrigerator or your screen at work that says "+2" or "Just breathe," or something to remind you to practice a couple of times a day. Also, if there is a time when you are feeling upset or stressed, try it and see what you notice. Sometimes, people feel calmer after doing this exercise and sometimes they don't—both are OK, just notice what your experience is. If it's not helpful, that's OK. Try some of the other strategies in this chapter.

NOTICING YOUR SENSES

This is an exercise that you can use to be present every day when you are going about your daily work or activities, while you are eating, spending time with others—really, any time. It's a practice of bringing your attention to your senses in the moment and noticing your sensory experiences in the moment. Visit https://ccfwb.uw.edu/resource/sensesmeditation/ to hear an audio recording of someone guiding you through the practice. Here's what you do:

- Get your body in an awake and holdable position. Start by sitting up straight and opening up our shoulders and chest. Keep your eyes open but look down about 3 or 4 feet in front of you. Take a deep, long breath in and out.
- Without moving your head or looking all around, bring your attention to what you can see in your setting, in the moment. Notice what you see. Do this for about 5 seconds.
- Notice something else that you can see. Notice one particular detail for a few seconds.
- Next, bring your attention to what you can hear. Notice the sounds you hear. Do this for about 5 seconds.
- Listen for something else, another sound you can hear. Notice one particular sound.
- Bring your attention to what you can smell. Notice any smells. Do this for about 5 seconds.
- Then, bring your attention to what you can feel on the skin of your hands or on your face and cheeks. Is there cool or warm air? A breeze?
- What can you feel touching your body? Your feet on the floor? Your seat on the chair? Pay attention to one thing you can feel on your body for about 5 seconds.
- Bring your attention to what you taste. Notice what you taste in your mouth and on your tongue.
- Now bring your attention back to what you can see. Notice what you see.
- Notice the sounds you hear.
- Notice any smells.
- Notice what you feel on your body or skin.

- Notice what you taste.
- Take a deep, long breath, and come back to the moment.

What did you notice? Was this different from how you normally notice things?

NOTICING YOUR CHILD

Often, when we are interacting with our children we are distracted by our phones or devices pinging us, thoughts of what we could or should be doing, or even the fact that we're not actually very interested in what our children are talking about or playing. Yet, we know our children crave our undivided attention and presence. Even if we aren't excited by what our children are playing or saying, we can be enthralled with who our children are and what they can do.

This is an exercise to help us to stay focused and participate in the moment when we are interacting with our child. This means noticing and engaging. What do you think we mean by "noticing"? When we practice being present, we are practicing observing things without judgment, without deciding if they are good or bad. We notice what is there, and we practice observing. Right now, we're going to talk about the steps for noticing and engaging mindfully with our children.

For the next exercise, we would like you to do one of two things. If you have a picture of your child with you (on your phone or in your wallet), you can look at that while doing a noticing practice. You could also close your eyes and bring up a recent memory of interacting with your child, a memory that you can bring up vividly and see your child. After you practice this a couple of times using a picture or your imagination, try it while you are playing with your child, for example, during Child-Led Time (see Chapter 10).

While looking at or thinking about your child, practice the following, pausing at each for about 5 seconds:

- Notice your child's eyes. Observe them.
- Notice your child's mouth.
- Notice your child's whole face.
- Observe your child's expression. Try to identify the feeling or emotion that is on your child's face. Don't try to figure out WHY they are feeling a certain feeling. And don't try to figure out HOW THEY SHOULD be feeling given other things that have recently happened. Right now, try to notice the feelings that are suggested by your child's facial expression.
- Observe your child's posture. What does posture tell you? Does it say anything about how your child might be feeling right now?
- Notice your child's breathing. Can you see your child's chest or stomach moving as she or he is breathing?
- Notice your child's hands, their size and shape, and what they are doing.
- Notice your child's ideas. If the memory involves, for example, a game you are playing with your child, notice the thoughts or ideas your child brings to the game. Notice your child's imagination or creativity in the game you are playing.
- For a moment, connect with your love and warmth for your child. Looking at your child, connect with the things you really enjoy about your child.
- Respond to your child. Remember to stay engaged. Your mind may wander. If it does, notice this and bring it back to your time with your child. Use active listening. Respond to your child's comments, ideas, and bids for your interaction with him or her. Follow your child's lead (see our discussion of Child-Led Time in Chapter 10). And go with the flow! Respond to

each of your child's next words or actions by following his or her lead.

- Now go back to the beginning. Go through the list again.
- Notice your child's eyes.
- Notice your child's mouth.
- Notice your child's whole face. Observe your child's expression. What feeling or emotion is suggested by your child's expression?
- Notice your child's posture. What does your child's posture tell you about how they are feeling?
- Notice your child breathing.
- Notice your child's hands, their size and shape, and what they are doing.
- Connect with your love for your child, and respond and go with the flow.

Does this practice help you stay focused on your child, paying attention in the moment while interacting with them? Does this help you notice how your child communicates their thoughts and feelings?

STRESS CHECK

This is a simple and effective exercise that tries to make us aware of the stress we hold in our body and notice it there. Science shows that accepting stress, tension, or pain in our bodies is more effective than trying to control them. It is also more relaxing. When we hold stress in our bodies . . . we might not even realize we're doing that . . . we bring that stress into our relationships and our work. Some people hold tension in their shoulders or neck or head, and that tension can affect almost everything we do.

Some of you might be familiar with stress management exercises that are like this. In those, you might notice your body parts and then just notice how they feel, or their heaviness or lightness. In this next exercise, we are going to call your attention to your muscles by tensing them and then releasing them. This is a great way to find where you are holding tension or stress in your body. When you tense your muscles and then release them, focus on how it feels to release them after tensing them. This lets you discover what it feels like to let go of tension in your body.

Here are a few pointers before beginning:

- When you do this at home, silence your cell phone. You may set a 5-minute alarm, but keep the volume low so you aren't startled when it goes off.
- Wear comfortable clothes. Lie on your back, or sit in a chair with both feet touching the floor.
- When thoughts distract, or when your mind wanders, gently and patiently notice it and return your attention to your breath and body.
- There are no expectations, and don't worry about doing it "right." You are doing it. There's nothing magical about this exercise—sometimes it's relaxing, and sometimes it's not. The point is to help us get into the moment we are experiencing right now as opposed to reliving the past or preparing for the future.

Let's begin. Visit https://ccfwb.uw.edu/resource/musclerelaxation to hear an audio recording of someone guiding you through the practice. Here's what you do:

- Get your body in an awake and holdable position. Start by sitting up straight and opening up your shoulders and chest. You can keep your eyes open, resting your gaze on the floor or table in front of you, or you can close your eyes if you prefer.

- Breathe in s-l-o-w-l-y and deeply through your nose. Feel your abdomen move outward as your diaphragm contracts and draws air into your lungs. Your chest should not rise noticeably.
- While breathing slowly, direct attention to your hands. Feel your hands. Clench your fist, then release it a few times, and notice how it feels to clench and how it feels to release. Rest your hands.
- Breathe in and out slowly, noticing your hands.
- If thoughts appear, that's fine. Gently come back to noticing your hands.
- Bring your attention to your arms. There might be heaviness, discomfort, or maybe nothing. Just notice what is there.
- Breathe in and tense your arms muscles, and gently direct attention to your arms. Breathe out and relax your arms and hands.
- Remain there with your attention on your hands and arms. Breathe.
- Now bring your attention to your shoulders and neck. Just notice your shoulders and neck. Raise and drop your shoulders a few times, and notice how it feels to raise and drop them.
- Breathe in and out, and relax your shoulders.
- Now, feel how your back rests against the chair/floor. Notice the chair/floor supporting your back.
- Breathe in and out, and notice your hands, then arms, then shoulders, and back again. Let them all rest or relax as much as possible.
- Just breathe; let any sensation come to you. Accept it as a part of you.
- Return your attention to your breathing. Take three more breaths, paying attention to your breath coming in and going out. Then come back to the moment.

You can do this breathing and awareness exercise for a few minutes at home. You can do it when you wake up, or at night, when you are in bed. You can also do it for a couple of minutes at work. You can include your whole body, starting with your feet and legs and including your face and head. It is a great way to deal with tension or anger in your body so you can calm down when you are in a heated or challenging situation. It's a great way to prepare yourself for interacting with your child in the most positive and effective way possible.

SELF-COMPASSION BREAK

To be effective in supporting our children when they are having challenging feelings or behaviors, we also need to be able to give ourselves support and caring. We want to introduce the idea and practice of self-compassion developed by Kristin Neff (2023). *Self-compassion* involves giving ourselves the same support and kindness and caring that we would give a friend.

There are three steps to a self-compassion break. The first step is acknowledging that a situation you might be experiencing is challenging, difficult, or painful. We need to acknowledge a situation and our emotions before we can decide what is needed. The second step is reminding ourselves that we are not alone—that other people have felt this way before or faced similar challenges. This is sometimes called our *common humanity*. The third and final step is extending kindness to ourselves. This is often done with a simple phrase we can say to ourselves. Essentially, we repeat what words of support we need to hear.

What are some phrases we tell our friends (or ourselves) when someone is going through a hard time? Let's phrase these as if we're telling ourselves. Some examples are "My best is good enough"; "This is hard, but I've gotten through hard times before"; "What will be, will be"; "I've done my best, let go of the rest."

We next present the steps involved in taking a self-compassion break. Visit https://ccfwb.uw.edu/resource/self-compassion-break-8-mins/

to hear an audio recording of someone guiding you through a self-compassion break. Here's what you do:

- Take a moment to get comfortable in your chair, perhaps inviting yourself to come into more of an awake position and sitting a bit taller. Rest your eyes on the table or floor in front of you, or you are welcome to close your eyes if you want.
- Take a moment to observe your breath. Do this for about 10 seconds.
- Now bring to mind a difficult situation you were in recently, or a time when you felt a strong emotion. Maybe you felt overwhelmed by work, or your child did something that upset you, or you had an argument with a family member. Reflect for about 10 seconds.
- Acknowledge the moment of difficulty. This can be as simple as a sentence such as "This is really stressful," or "This hurts," or "This was hard." Find a phrase that works for you and repeat it silently for about 10 seconds.
- Now find a way to connect with the common experiences we all can have—our common humanity. This could be a sentence such as "I'm not alone. Others have felt this way, too." Find a phrase that feels true for you and repeat it silently for about 10 seconds.
- For these last few steps, it can be helpful to place your hand over your heart for extra grounding. A few other options people like are holding yourself in a hug, folding one hand over the other in your lap, or using one thumb to gently massage the opposite wrist or arm. There might be something you do intuitively when you need support. Take a moment to see what feels grounding to you.
- Now extend kindness to yourself. Ask yourself, what do I need now? What do I need to hear? This might be a sentence such

as "Remember to be patient," "Remember to take the rest I need," or "I am good enough."
- If it feels difficult to find a phrase, think about what you would say to comfort a friend who is going through this situation. Once you find your phrase, repeat it two or three times silently.
- With your next two or three breaths, bring your attention back to the moment.

This is a helpful practice you can do anytime. One example for when it can help is when you feel like you can't stop thinking about something, or when you are thinking about something you didn't handle very well. This can be an in-the-moment practice to help you switch gears. If you came up with a helpful phrase you can say to be kind to yourself when you are having a difficult experience, write it down on a notecard or sticky note. Try taking a "self-compassion break" a couple of times a week.

WISE MIND

Although we talk about all of the various parenting skills individually, some of the practices complement each other. There are two important skills in making wise, effective choices as parents. To engage in wise, effective parenting, especially in challenging situations, we have to be able to be aware of our own reasons, goals, and emotions, and we have to be aware of our children's reasons, goals, and emotions. We do this using two skills. We examine and balance our own reasons and emotions using a skill called *Wise Mind*. We use Wise Mind to help us decide what our children need and what we can do to be effective. This will help us with the second skill, *being balanced*. In this, we learn how to balance providing structure and guidance with supporting our children's autonomy or independence. We talk about being balanced in Chapter 12. Here, we describe practicing Wise Mind.

The practice of Wise Mind was created by Marsha Linehan (2015), who developed a type of therapy called dialectical behavioral therapy. Wise Mind is a skill for being present and being balanced. Wise Mind means being in the moment, and taking a moment, to tap into the wisdom inside you when you are working with your child or having a challenging interaction with your child. It's about taking a moment to check your own wisdom or intuition about what is the best thing to do to help your child in that moment. Wise Mind is a way of guiding you about when to step in and when to step back, by asking yourself "What is needed? What will be effective?" To understand Wise Mind, we have to understand three states of mind: Emotion Mind, Rational Mind, and Wise Mind (see Figure 9.1).

When you hear *Emotion Mind*, what comes to mind to you? What do you think it means? Yes, Emotion Mind is when you are ruled by emotions, feelings, and mood. Some examples of when your emotions or moods rule your actions include when you're so angry you say things you didn't mean or hurtful things, you want a cookie so badly you eat one even if you know you shouldn't, and you're so scared you back out of doing something you know you should do.

What about *Rational Mind*—what comes to mind? Yes, this is when you are ruled by facts, logic, and pragmatics. Some examples

FIGURE 9.1. Wise Mind

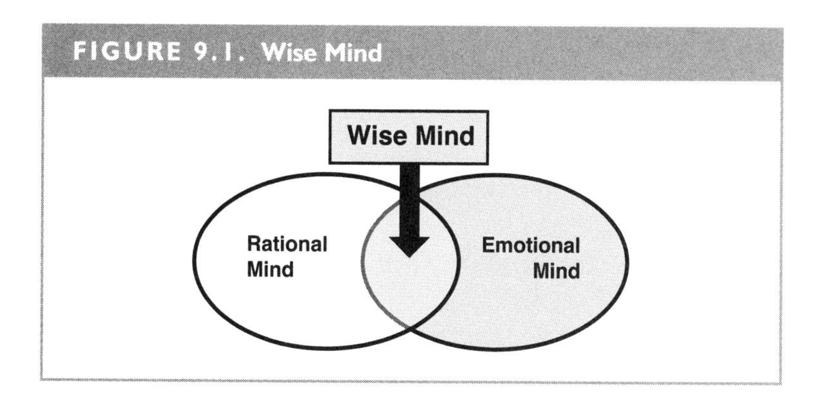

of using your Rational Mind include focusing on the plans of an outing so much you don't really enjoy the moment and being so focused on solving a problem that you forget to acknowledge someone's feelings.

What would it be like if you only lead your life in Rational Mind—if you were like Dr. Spock from Star Trek? Or like a computer? What would be good about that? What would be missing? You would be organized, planful, and reasonable in solving problems, but maybe missing joy and empathy.

What would it be like if you only lead your life from Emotion Mind—what would that look like? What would be good? What would you be missing? You would be passionate and feel life deeply, but maybe impulsive, engaging in hurtful behaviors toward yourself or others, and hurting your relationships.

Clearly, it doesn't work to be all of either one, and that's where the concept of Wise Mind comes in! The balance or combination between Emotion Mind and Rational Mind is Wise Mind. Wise Mind recognizes both: You have an emotion about something and you grasp the reality or pragmatics of the situation. Wise Mind involves tapping into your inner wisdom that comes when you balance reason and emotion.

The goal is NOT to be in Wise Mind all the time! It's impossible. But there are times when we want to GET INTO Wise Mind, especially around our parenting. For example, Wise Mind is great for making parenting decisions because it honors both your emotion (Emotion Mind) in a situation and the logistics of a situation (Rational Mind). Both emotions and reason are required to make our most wise decisions.

Wise Mind is the place where our Rational Mind and our Emotional Mind overlap. It is the balance of the two, the "middle way." Wise Mind is a deep sense of intuitive knowing that goes beyond reason and emotion. It is a sense of knowing or intuition about what is needed in a situation, what will be an effective thing to do in a situation. *The goal of Wise Mind is to make the best, most effective decision in that moment.* In Wise Mind, we ask ourselves, "What is needed? What will be effective?"

We all have wisdom within us. At first, we might not believe that, or we might not feel that way. But our intuition, or our gut feeling, or our inner sense does provide us with some guidance and wisdom. And we can learn to pay attention to it. As with anything we do for the first time or first few times, we might not be great at tapping into our inner wisdom. With time and practice, though, we can begin to access our Wise Mind.

We all experience Wise Mind in different ways. Wise Mind might feel like intuition inside you, in a quiet space within you, where you just know something is right or true. It is a part of each person that can know and experience something as true or valid. It is a quiet, calm place inside you, where you are centered. For some, it is a still, small voice within that knows what is best. For others, Wise Mind is experienced as a gut feeling of what the best course of action to take is. Take a minute to imagine or remember this experience of Wise Mind and how you feel it inside yourself. Can you recall an experience of feeling this place of Wise Mind in making a decision, parenting or otherwise? What did it feel like?

We all have the capacity to access our Wise Mind. But we don't always listen to it. As with any new skill, we need practice to access Wise Mind, and when we practice and attempt to act from Wise Mind often enough, it becomes more natural.

Most of us have had the experience that we know we could have handled a situation differently, more effectively, than we did—and we realize it after the fact. Usually, we realize that because, after a situation is done, we can have a balance of perspective and emotion. We've heard the saying that "hindsight is 20/20." Sometimes, we see things more clearly, with a more balanced perspective, when we look back on it or when we give ourselves some time or distance. Tapping into Wise Mind is intended to help us have that perspective and balance in the situation when it's happening so we can make choices with 20/20 foresight instead of hindsight.

When we talk about Wise Mind, we are talking about tapping into our own wisdom inside us. Picture a water well that you can dip into to draw up the wisdom inside you. Everyone has a Wise Mind, but it's not always accessible to us.

You can try to access our wisdom by doing this exercise:

- Sit in a holdable position, with our shoulders and chest open and your eyes either looking down in front of you or closed, whichever you prefer.
- Wise Mind is the practice of accessing the wisdom within each of us. The wisdom is deep within us, in a quiet, still place, like a room or an open space that is still, peaceful, and quiet. We sometimes don't reach deeply inside ourselves to access it.
- Notice your breath, as it goes in and out for about two or three breaths.
- Take a long, slow breath. With your next couple of breaths, follow your breath as it enters your nose; follow it into your lungs; and follow it into a still, quiet place deep inside you.
- Rest in that place deep inside yourself for a few breaths.
- Imagine or feel where your wisdom might be in that place inside you. Imagine walking into a deep part of yourself, like walking down steps or through corridors into a peaceful, still, comfortable, and quiet place.
- It might not be easy to find the deepest places where your wisdom resides. There might be false turns or locked doors. You might need to find a key to open the door. Take a minute to imagine traveling or walking deep within yourself to find the place of your wisdom.

- Wise Mind is sometimes experienced in the center of the body (belly), or in the center of the head, or between the eyes. Sometimes a person can find it by following the breath in and out, or in the moment between the end of your breath in and your breath out. Sit in that still, quiet place deep inside you for a couple more minutes.
- Bring your attention back to the present moment.

If we can find this quiet, still place or state we can tap into our own resource or well of wisdom. And, like learning to ride a bike, at first it's really hard, but once you have practiced it will come more naturally and more easily.

Finding your Wise Mind isn't anything mystical or magical. When we practice tapping into Wise Mind, we are giving ourselves a chance to reflect and let an answer to our situation come out of our own wisdom. It's a way of pausing, holding our feelings and thoughts, observing them, not judging or trying to control them but holding them together and balancing them. When we can observe our thoughts and feelings without judging them, but instead balancing them, we can draw a Wise-Minded response from our well of wisdom. Remember, *the goal of Wise Mind is to make the best, most effective decision in that moment.*

We now present two exercises to help use Wise Mind when we are interacting with our children. The first one is called "Be in the Pauses." Visit https://ccfwb.uw.edu/resource/beinthepause/ to hear an audio recording of someone guiding you through the exercise. Here's what you do:

- As you engage in mindful breathing, allow yourself to notice the pause after each inhalation and each exhalation. It may be slight, but it's there. This pause is much like the still space that exists when changing directions on a swing. Think of pushing your child on a swing, noticing the pause as they swing forward and back. Our breath has a similar pause between inhaling and exhaling.

- Notice the stillness within each pause. Allow yourself to find awareness in the pauses at the top and bottom of each breath. Settle in to each pause and find stillness within.
- See if you can extend the pause slightly, holding it just a second longer.
- Using the image you developed in the Wise Mind exercise described earlier, try to access the place of your wisdom in the stillness between breaths.

The second exercise is called "Breathe 'Wise' In, Breathe 'Mind' Out." This exercise is particularly helpful if you feel stuck in Emotion Mind and are feeling overwhelmed. In these moments, it may be difficult to focus your attention on a longer visualization exercise. At times like this, simply notice that you are feeling intense emotions and begin to direct your focus toward your breath. Visit https://ccfwb.uw.edu/resource/wise-mind-breathing-5-minutes/ to hear an audio recording of someone guiding you through this exercise. Here's what you do:

- As you pull the air into your lungs, say the word "wise" in your mind. As the air leaves your lungs, say the word "mind" to yourself.
- The idea is to focus your attention entirely on these words as you breathe in and out to begin to settle yourself back into a place of calm and wisdom.
- Using the image you developed in the exercise presented earlier, try to access the place of your wisdom with each breath in and out.

You can see that if you use Wise Mind in interactions with your children, especially in challenging ones, it helps you to do two very important things. First, you need to stop: Using Wise Mind helps us not to act immediately, but to pause. Second, you use your breathing to tap into your Wise Mind, so you can use your Wise Mind Breathing here, which also helps us calm down.

Try this exercise as you think about a challenging situation with your child:

- Think about something that has been a struggle or a challenge or that led to a heated exchange with your child recently. Think about what your child did and then what you did.
- Try one of the Wise Mind Breathing exercises. Pick the one you liked better: Be in the Pauses or Breathe "Wise" In, Breathe "Mind" Out. As you imagine the challenging situation, take four or five breaths doing either Be in the Pauses or Breathe "Wise" In, Breathe "Mind" Out.
- With your next few breaths, ask yourself, "What is needed? What is effective in this situation?"
- In the pauses between breaths, let your Wise Mind answer, "What is needed? What is effective?" Do this for three or four breaths.
- With one or two more breaths, come back to the moment. What did you experience? How did that go? What happened when you reflected on a problem with Wise Mind?

EMOTION REGULATION IN DIFFICULT SITUATIONS

The next few strategies are intended to help you deal with situations that are heated. To handle these situations effectively, we need to be able to manage our own emotions and reactions toward our children. Every parent has had moments that weren't their best parenting moments. We look back on how we handled something and know that we could have done it differently, or we just lost control of our emotions and behaviors and said or did things that made the situation worse instead of better. We didn't bring our best self to the situation.

It happens to all of us, and it happens to the best of us. Sometimes stress or challenges in our lives put us on edge or make us impatient, and then something that happens with our children can be the last straw. We might yell. We might disengage entirely, leaving our children alone to deal with a difficult feeling or situation. We might say something that is critical or hurtful. Or sometimes we lash out physically, grabbing our children or hitting them.

We know from years of research that those responses can make our children's behaviors worse. Over time, it contributes to them doing worse in school and worse with friends. It can increase their anxiety and depression. And it can lead to more oppositional and problem behaviors at school and at home. So, our goal here is to introduce strategies for parents to manage their own stress, distress, sadness, and anger successfully, so that when there is a heated or emotional situation with their child they will be able to be more effective in handling it.

PAUSING TO SEE THINGS MORE CLEARLY

If you have a snow globe at home, bring it out (or you can watch a video of a snow globe if you don't).

- Look at a snow globe. When you shake it up, what do you see? The snow looks like turmoil or a storm, and you can't see clearly through the snow globe or see what's inside it.
- Now, watch it as it settles down. As you're watching, also notice your breathing, just breathing, and watching the snow settle.

- What did you feel while you were watching the snow globe? As the snow settles, it starts to look and feel a little calmer, and you can see more clearly.

Just like with a snow globe, when we give ourselves just a few seconds or so to calm down when we are upset with our children, we are more likely to be able to see the situation more clearly, understand and validate our children's feelings, and to make a wise decision about what would be an effective way to handle the situation.

You can use a snow globe or a sand timer at home to help you calm down. You can focus on how the snow is settling or how the sand in a timer is dropping while you practice your +2 Breathing.

STOP

Getting a hold of our emotions is an important first step in interacting with our children, especially in heated or challenging situations. It's important that we are responding to our children and not reacting from our emotions. We want to bring our best selves to the situation. One skill for this is STOP. We've already presented all the skills you use in STOP, and the STOP practice helps us put it all together in a challenging situation. The four steps of STOP are as follows:

1. Stop. Pause before responding or reacting.
2. Take 1 or 2 breaths. Use +2 Breathing, breathing in deeply and breathing out a little longer than you breathe in.
3. Observe. Notice yourself and your child. Notice your own body and feelings and thoughts. Then look at your child or the person you are interacting with, and notice their eyes, face, and posture, noticing what they might be feeling.
4. Proceed Wisely. Check your Wise Mind for an effective course of action and proceed. Use either Be in the Pauses or Breathe "Wise" in, Breathe "Mind"out to access Wise Mind. Hold

your emotions and reasons in mind for a few seconds and breaths. Ask yourself, "What is needed? What will be effective?" Be intentional; consider the goal: What is the aim of the next thing you say or do? Be effective versus being right.

PARENT TIME-OUT

Sometimes, we are still so charged with emotion—sad, overwhelmed, angry, frustrated, hurt, annoyed—that it's not enough to just pause for one or two breaths and observe or to hold ourselves for a few seconds. Sometimes, we need to calm down even more before proceeding. In those situations, we can take a Parent Time-Out and try something else to calm down. We usually think of time-out as something we use for our children. But we can also benefit from time-outs ourselves.

The goal of Parent Time-Out is not to escape the situation or disengage. The goal is to give yourself some time to get in a state that allows you to bring your best self to the situation.

If you need a Parent Time-Out, tell your child something like this:

> I am feeling frustrated or upset right now. I love you and want to respond to you in the best way I can. Right now, I need a few minutes to calm down so that I can handle this situation in the best way possible. I am going to take a short time-out, and then I will be back in a few minutes.

In Parent Time-Out, we remove ourselves from the situation for a few minutes.

1. Go in another room and try using STOP again.
2. Try +2 Breathing.
3. Try Wise Mind Breathing.
4. Try moving around or listening to music.

5. Try drinking water.
6. Try doing a stress check.
7. Try some vigorous exercise, like doing 20 to 30 jumping jacks or lunges.
8. Take a deep breath, then another two.

Try any of the mindfulness and emotion regulation practices from this chapter to support being present and bringing your best self to each interaction with your child. Make a plan to use one or two of these. Pick the one or two that might work best for you.

Prepare yourself with a plan. If those don't work, next time try different ones. Once you've done this, make a plan for how you will approach the situation, checking your Wise Mind for the most effective way to handle it, and then go back and re-engage, addressing the situation. If you don't have a quiet place to go, you can also ask your child to give you 1 or 2 minutes of quiet space, even if you're all in the same room.

Now let's talk about when and how to use STOP and Parent Time-Out strategies. The first thing to do is to notice when we start getting upset. We might be getting angry or frustrated, or distressed or sad. We might start to feel it in our stomach, or in our head, or as tension in our neck and shoulders. If we can catch our emotions as they are just starting, we might be able to manage our feelings so we can remain effective in the situation.

Let's see if we can figure out where you start feeling your negative emotions when they arise:

- Close your eyes and think about the most recent time that you were really upset—either stressed or distressed or angry or sad. Imagine the situation in which you were feeling that way.
- For a few seconds, imagine yourself feeling that way right now.
- Where in your body are you feeling that emotion?

- Take a few seconds to check your body and figure out where you are feeling the emotion.
- Now take a couple deep breaths and come back to the moment. Where did you feel your emotions? How did you know you were feeling those emotions?

You can practice noticing in yourself when your emotions start to arise, starting with knowing where you feel your emotions in your body. When an emotion starts to arise in a heated situation with your child, you can notice it early and use STOP together with one of the other calming-down strategies.

Try to practice using STOP with either +2 Breathing or Wise Mind Breathing. Pick whichever one you prefer.

1. Close your eyes and imagine the same situation you just imagined in the exercise we just presented. Remember the situation that you were thinking about, a situation in which you were really upset.
2. Start to feel your emotions arising in your body. Take a few seconds to notice where you start to feel your emotions.
3. When you start to feel the emotion from the situation, say to yourself "STOP."
4. Take 2 breaths.
5. Observe. Notice where in your body you feel the feelings or feel upset.
6. Now try the strategy you picked—+2 Breathing or Wise Mind Breathing—for a few seconds. Do this for four or five breaths.
7. Now take a couple of deep breaths and come back to the moment. What did you experience? How did it go?

These skills take practice, so do them a couple times during the week, especially when you notice yourself getting tense, upset, or frustrated.

CONCLUSION

When we cultivate our capacity to be present in the moment, to notice and observe without making assumptions or judgments, and to be calm and effective, we are more likely to bring our best selves to our interactions with our children. We can make wise choices for handling difficult situations, bringing awareness to both our own emotional reactions and those of our children. Some of the suggested techniques may not feel right to you, but if you give these a try you should be able to identify some that are a good fit. Of course, there are other practices available online, and you may benefit from practicing yoga, or consulting with a behavioral or mental health specialist with relevant expertise. By being present with our children, we communicate to them that we value being with them, and we model compassion toward others and toward oneself.

CHAPTER 10

BE WARM

In this chapter, we introduce some practices that, research shows, increase the positive quality of the parent–child relationship. They are aimed at helping children feel accepted, supported, and valued. Although we frame these practices as interactions with your child, you can practice them in other relationships as well.

ACCEPTANCE AND AFFECTION

For children to feel accepted, supported, and valued, they need to hear authentic compliments and praise from their parents, and in this chapter we suggest some simple ways to build those in during Child-Led Time and, in Chapter 12, with Notice the Good. Of course, you can feel free to sprinkle these in liberally at other times as well. Research suggests that people need to hear four positive inputs for every negative input about their behavior, and this is particularly true for our children.

Being warm also refers to showing affection verbally and nonverbally. This might take the form of spontaneous expressions of love and pride, a hug, an arm around the shoulder, or holding hands. We recognize that the ways parents show their acceptance and affection for their children might look different in different families and cultures, so we encourage you to build practices that fit your family.

ACTIVE LISTENING

Active Listening is a starting point for all of the other parenting tools. It actually is listening in a particular way—with intention and actively. In Active Listening, we are listening with our whole mind and body, with focused attention. And we are *intentionally showing* the other person that we are listening. How do we do that? Think about how you know when someone is listening to you. They are doing things like making eye contact; leaning in; nodding; making verbalizations that indicate interest and understanding—like "Uh-huh" and "OK"; not interrupting or taking over the conversation; and encouraging the person to keep talking, not planning ahead what they want to say or anticipating what the speaker is going to say.

Can you think of how someone can listen that is not Active Listening—not in the moment with the intention of understanding? What are some passive or inactive ways of listening? They might include things like doing something else while someone is talking, looking around, interrupting, referring the topic back to themselves, being on the phone or computer while someone is talking to them, and forgetting the train of the conversation if there is a disruption. How does it feel when you are trying to tell someone something important and they engage in these passive listening behaviors? It feels like they aren't listening and that what you are saying is not valued. Pause for a moment and think: How many times have you done some of these things while your child is trying to talk with you? We can't be listening actively all of the time! But we can be intentional about tuning in and leaning in to listen to our children sometimes, ideally at least once or twice a day.

Active Listening is quietly listening, without interrupting or talking over someone. We are showing the other person that we are listening by

- looking them in the eye (if this is how your culture shows engagement);

- leaning in with interest;
- nodding when appropriate;
- saying "OK," or "Uh-huh," or "I see" when appropriate;
- asking the person to "go on," or "say more," or "tell me more"; and
- not interrupting or talking over them.

Try this simple active listening exercise with someone. Make sure you frame this as an exercise or experiment to see how it feels when a person listens actively or passively.

- Tell each other about your day. Tell your partner about your day, giving details from when you woke up through the day. Each person will take turns being the listener and the speaker for 1 minute, then switch.
- For the first 30 seconds, the listener should break all the rules of actively listening: Don't look the person in the eyes, don't lean in, don't nod, do look around, check your phone, and do interrupt a few times. After 30 seconds, switch and start listening actively. Then follow all the rules of Active Listening.
- After a minute, switch roles. The listener becomes the speaker, and the speaker is now the listener.
- What did you think of that? What did you notice? How did it feel when the person was breaking the listening rules? How was it different when the person was using Active Listening?
- Think about how this applies to how you listen to your child.

CHILD-LED TIME

The following exercise, Child-Led Time, is adapted from one created by R. J. McMahon and R. L. Forehand (2003, adaptation in Lengua, 2015). Child-Led Time is a particular way of spending time with your child that builds a positive relationship. This is a time that you set aside every day with your child. It can be 20 minutes a day, but if it's hard to find 20 minutes, it can be 10 or 15 minutes a day. Even 5 minutes a day can make a difference. Every day, at about the same time, at a convenient time when you have nothing urgent you need to do, you sit down and play with your child. Your child gets to pick what you'll play, and your child gets to lead the play time—that's why it's called "Child-Led Time."

There are three goals of Child-Led Time:

1. **Practice participating in the moment.** It's a chance for you to practice your Be Present skills of noticing and engaging mindfully.
2. **Enjoy your child.** It's a time to make note of all the great qualities of your child—their smile, beautiful face and eyes, ideas, laughter. This time is a chance for you to connect with your love for your child and build your bond and positive relationship with your child. This bond can be the foundation for a close and positive relationship for years to come. And you can do this with just 10 to 20 minutes set aside for your child every day.
3. **Notice your child's good behaviors and qualities.** Child-Led Time is a chance to start paying attention to your child's successes, skills, positive behaviors, and the times they actually are doing the things you want them to do, like being polite, focused, persistent, well-behaved, and calm.

First, let's focus on practicing participating in the moment, connecting with your love for your child and noticing your child's face, facial expressions and emotions during Child-Led Time. In Chapter 9, we introduced the "Noticing Your Child" skill. When you set aside this time to be with your child, also use the time to practice being present or mindful in the moment.

Child-Led Time is a great way to practice being present. It is also a very effective tool for building a warm, connected, positive relationship with your child. It's a chance to get to know your child's thoughts and emotions more deeply. It's a time to really enjoy your child and pay attention to how much you love your child.

Child-Led Time is a particular WAY of playing with your child. It's playing with your child in a way that lets your child feel special, the focus of your attention, and it lets your child feel important because they get to be in charge. Your child gets to pick what you will play together and gets to lead the play time. Think about your child's day-to-day life. How many times do they get to be in charge, where they get to decide what happens? Usually, adults are making decisions for them and directing what they do. So what's really special about Child-Led Time is that your child gets to guide the plan.

Now think about how many of us really focus and play with our children. How many of us have felt like it's hard to sit and play with our kids? The great thing about Child-Led Time is that there are some guidelines or rules for doing it, and we just have to follow our children's lead. We just play what they prompt us to play. So even if we feel like we might not be very good at playing with our kids, we can just follow our children's lead.

Child-Led Time has some very specific guidelines that we should use. Most important is that your child picks the activity. Your child may pick a game or activity that you're not particularly fond of. But remember that this is a chance for your child to be in charge, to do what they want, and to build their relationship with you. Even if you don't really enjoy the activity, try to enjoy your child. We'll talk about that in a minute.

It is a good idea, however, to avoid activities that are competitive (e.g., games in which one person wins) and activities during which it is hard to have good interactions (e.g., watching a movie or playing a video game). Providing your child with some options for activities, such as blocks, LEGOs, drawing, puzzles, playing catch, taking a walk, playing outside, cards or board games, or reading together will ensure that whatever choice is made you will be able to engage in high-quality interactions.

Another important guideline is that your child leads the activity. They get to decide how the activity goes. Just like playing follow-the-leader, you do what your child does, or you do what your child asks you to do. The most important part is to go with the flow. Try not to make negative or critical comments. Try not to point out things that are wrong or not how you would do it. Just go with it. In order for your child to truly lead, there are a few rules for this special time:

- **No instructions or commands.** During this time, your child is deciding what to do and leading the direction of the interaction. Unless there is a safety issue, or your child is being very inappropriate (in which case you should pause your Child-Led Time for a few minutes), you should be careful to avoid giving instructions.
- **No judgments.** You may notice during Child-Led Time that your child says or does things that seem goofy, odd, or confusing. This is a perfect time to practice mindfulness and just observe and reflect, without attaching a judgment to what your child is doing.
- **Ignore minor misbehavior.** What is "minor" versus "major" is decided by each family. Talking loudly, running around, and acting silly or wild might be ignored during Child-Led Time. Major misbehaviors, though, usually include being aggressive or destructive. In these cases, parents can say that if the child is not able to play respectfully or use the play materials appropriately, then the play will stop. Because children pick the activity, most often this redirection will be effective. If it's not, the activity needs to be stopped, with an invitation for a similar

interaction later, when the child is able to engage appropriately. This does not mean that you need to discontinue Child-Led Time altogether. You can return to it with another activity that is less likely to result in aggressive or destructive behavior.

While you are doing the activity with your child, be present. Here is where you practice noticing and engaging mindfully. Your child's eyes, facial expressions, posture, gestures, ideas, and play are all windows into their inner lives, their emotions and thoughts. During Child-Led Time, you are most likely to see your child in a happy, relaxed state. Sit close, offer physical affection as appropriate, make eye contact, smile. Here you can use the Noticing your Child mindfulness practice described in Chapter 9. Notice your child's eyes, mouth, whole face, and expression. What feeling or emotion is suggested by your child's expression? Notice your child's posture. What does your child's posture tell you about how they are feeling? Notice your child breathing. Connect with your love for your child, and respond and go with the flow. We want to really notice this and get to know our child during these times, so we can also see when they are not in a calm state at other times. It helps us recognize more easily when they are upset at other times.

And of course, enjoy your child! Use Child-Led Time to connect with your love for your child and your enjoyment of your child. Because your child gets to pick the activity and lead the interaction, they will likely be in a relaxed, happy state. This is a chance to enjoy that part of your child. As you practice noticing, also enjoy your child's eyes, smile, thoughts, ideas, voice. Find shared interests and shared ideas. Appreciate who your child is, what is unique about your child, the qualities that are great about your child.

- Reflect on what your child is doing (e.g., "You are playing with the blocks"; "You put the red block on top of the blue block!";

"Wow, what a big tower!"; "You're making your dolls dance"; or "You are sitting very still"). If you are not used to reflecting on your child's activities in this manner, it may seem awkward or unnatural at first. This is to be expected. This kind of conversation is reminiscent of how sports broadcasters report on the game in their play-by-play commentary and can quickly become a new habit.

- Show that you are interested (e.g., "Oh! You built an airplane! Very creative.")
- Let your child know you are enjoying your time with them ("I'm really enjoying our special play time," "I'm having fun playing with you.")
- Sometimes, mimic what your child is doing. If they are playing with a doll, you can also play with a doll. If they are drawing a picture of a flower, you may also draw a picture of a flower. Be careful here to truly mimic and not to, for example, draw a perfect picture of a flower. Your flower and their flower should look similar.

Child-Led Time doesn't always go smoothly or as planned, and there are a few challenges that can come up. Often, children are having so much fun, they complain or become upset when the play time is up. If you are able to consistently have Child-Led Time with your child, especially if it is done at about the same time every day, this should dissipate over time. Your child will come to recognize that this is not a rare event but a regular thing, and you can remind them of that. Also, although it can be hard, complaining or disappointment at the end of Child-Led Time are also a sign of how much your child loves spending time with you. When you frame it that way, you might feel less bad about it. You can tell your child that you really enjoy spending this time with them too, and that you look forward to doing it again the next time.

Sometimes, your child may pick a game but doesn't play by the rules of the game. In Child-Led Time, your child gets to decide what to play and how to play it. The main rule is that you follow their lead. If your child makes up new rules or a new way to play, you can comment on it, noticing "Looks like you're coming up with a new way to play—teach it to me." The one caveat would be if your child is playing in a way that is cheating or disrespectful, you might want to ask them to play fairly or pick something else to play that is fair. It is also possible that your child becomes emotionally distressed during Child-Led Time, maybe because they are frustrated by what they have chosen to do (e.g., their drawing is not turning out the way they wanted). You can suggest that you pause Child-Led Time, help your child calm down, and then resume playing, allowing the child to decide what to play. If your child becomes so upset that emotional distress turns into aggressive or destructive actions, this is a sign that Child-Led Time is over for now. You can let your child know, when calmer interactions resume, that this special opportunity will return, predictably based on whatever frequency you are able to provide: "We can do this again tomorrow. Remember, we play games you pick as long as you are respectful."

To summarize, during Child-Led Time, as you are practicing being present, noticing and engaging mindfully, know that this is a chance to look through a window into your child's emotions, thoughts, ideas, and personality. Use these times to connect with your love for and enjoyment of your child. Enjoy your child's smile, thoughts, ideas, voice. Find interests that you connect on. Appreciate who your child is—the qualities that are great about your child. Remember to just follow your child's lead! Don't try to change what your child is doing. Just go with the flow.

Child-Led Time also presents an opportunity to practice being balanced and being consistent. One of the parenting practices we suggest is to Be Balanced: Step-In–Step Back, or Scaffolding. This means supporting, structuring, and guiding your child's play and work when needed as well as letting your child be independent and autonomous when they are doing fine without your help. It means balancing being helpful with letting your child be independent.

Child-Led Time is a chance to practice this. When you follow your child's lead, you let your child assert their desires or needs. Your child gets to decide what to play, and how (as long as their behavior is appropriate and safe). Your job is just to follow and go with the flow. That is supporting autonomy or independence.

Finally, we can also use Child-Led Time to practice being consistent. One way we start building a sense of safety and predictability for our children is by being consistent in spending Child-Led Time with them. Remember, it doesn't have to be a lot of time, 10 to 20 minutes a day, but it is important that they can count on it happening almost every day and at about the same time every day.

Another way we can practice being consistent during Child-Led Time is by noticing the things our children are doing that we WANT them to be doing. So many times, we point out their mistakes or misbehavior. It's a lot harder, and takes a lot of practice, to start noticing their successes, their desirable behaviors, and when they are meeting our expectations! So, we can use Child-Led Time to start practicing Notice the Good (see Chapter 12).

You can use Child-Led Time to notice desirable, expected behaviors, such as sitting, focusing, being careful with toys, being gentle while playing a physical game, and other things like that. Comment on these. You can say things like, "You are smiling right now. I like your smile"; "I like your idea about having the Barbies slide down a slide; it's fun!"; "You are sitting so calmly. It's nice to sit and play like this."

VALIDATION

One time to use our Be Present strategies is when we feel a distressing emotion arising in ourselves. However, we also want to be prepared to support our children when there is a difficult or heated interaction or when our children are having difficult emotions. In these situations, we want to notice how our child is feeling or behaving. Most of the time, our children give us cues that they are starting to get upset. We can notice or observe when our child looks distressed or sad or frustrated or angry. Remember, we've been noticing how they look when we are engaging in Child-Led Time. At those times, they should look calm and happy and content. Notice when they are *not* looking calm or content.

Think about one or two things you notice about your child when they are getting emotional or upset. Remember a time when your child was really mad or sad or upset. Picture your child's face and behaviors. Think about something in your child's facial expression or body or voice that tells you that they are getting upset. What are some of these things?

When we notice our children getting upset, we can use a skill called *validation* to really listen to our children to understand their reasons and emotions, to affirm their thoughts and feelings, and to help us figure out "What is needed? What will be effective?" Validation means confirming or verifying that a person's thoughts or feelings are valid. We aren't necessarily saying that we agree with them or even that their behaviors or actions are OK. In fact, we can understand why someone is feeling a certain way even when we disagree with them. Can you think of an example of understanding someone's negative feelings even if you don't agree? For example, your child might be angry that you made them stop playing a video game because the family rule is they have to stop 30 minutes before going to bed. You can understand why your child is angry—they were about to get to the next level and had to stop while they were invested in the game—while knowing that it was time to stop.

Validation involves finding the kernel of truth in others' experience or perspective by communicating that we can see how and why they feel or think what they think. We are affirming that our children's thoughts and feelings are valid in the situation, even if we don't agree with them.

One way to think of validation is to think of the "AND" in the situation, instead of the "BUT." When we say "but" to someone, we're saying that their thoughts and feelings are invalid. If we say, "I know you're upset, BUT what you did is wrong, and I'm upset too," we are implying that only one person's feelings, yours or mine, can be "right." When we say and mean the same thing with "AND"—"I know you're upset, AND what you did is wrong, and I'm upset too"—we can acknowledge that both of us are upset and both of our thoughts and feelings are present and understood. By thinking in terms of AND, we are acknowledging the truth in our child's thoughts and feelings and the truth in our thoughts and feelings—and that both things can be true at the same time.

Validation is an act of compassion—you try to understand how someone is feeling and see their perspective. To be effective with our children, we first must acknowledge their feelings, showing empathy or compassion for how they feel. When we do this, our children can move on more quickly from their hurt feelings and move into resolving the situation. When we validate, we listen actively in the moment, with the intention of understanding. When we validate, we listen, reflect, and connect.

- **Listen:**
  - Pay attention (remember to use active listening).
  - Give your child your undivided attention.
  - Look at your child—observe mindfully.
  - Encourage—lean in, nod, say "Yes," or "Uh-huh," or "Go on."
  - Defer judgment—don't interrupt or prepare your response or rebuttal as you are listening; it's OK to pause at the end to think of your response.

- **Reflect:**
  - Check your understanding by restating, paraphrasing, or summarizing: "What I'm hearing is . . ." or "It sounds like you are feeling . . ."
  - Comment on nonverbal cues: "You look really mad . . ." "Your body looks very tense . . ."
  - Clarify by asking questions: "What did you mean when you said . . ." or "Is this what you mean?"
- **Connect:**
  - Help your child connect and clarify the cause of the feeling, saying something like, "When this happened, you felt . . ." or "When I said this, you thought . . ."
  - Affirm that you can understand how the thought or feeling arose from the situation.

Consider this interaction. A parent brings her child to the park and directs the child to go play on the climber. There are a lot of kids on the climber, and the child hesitates and tells his mother that he doesn't want to play.

Child: I don't want to go.
Parent: I brought you all the way to the park because you said you wanted to play. [Sits facing out and away.]
Child: Will you go with me?
Parent: Just go play. What's up? Just go have fun. [Pushes child away, gently.]
Child: I'm scared. I don't want to go alone.
Parent: Scared of what? You come here all the time. Now you're just being silly. [Makes a critical face and shakes head.]

What happened in that interaction? What was the listener doing? What actions were invalidating? The parent dismisses the child's feeling of being scared rather than listening to understand what was leading to those feelings.

When we act in an invalidating way, we dismiss or criticize our children's thoughts, feelings, and experiences. We say that there is no reason for their thoughts and feelings, or that they are wrong to think and feel that way. We are also letting them know that they are not valuable to us because their thoughts and feelings, the things they need to say, are not worth listening to. In this interaction, the parent might have responded with validation something like this:

Child: I'm scared. I don't want to go alone.
Parent: Tell me what scares you about going to play.
Child: Someone might push me, and I could fall, or someone might make fun of me. I don't like that there are so many kids here.
Parent: I see, you are worried someone might push you or make fun of you. Those can be scary things. It probably won't happen, but if it does, what can you do to avoid being pushed?
Child: Maybe just not get too close to people.
Parent: And what about being teased? Could you come get me if that happens?
Child: Maybe.
Parent: Give it a try. Go and play. I'll be right here, and I'll be watching the whole time. I'll come over if it looks like you need me.

When we validate our children, we are letting them know that we are listening, that we understand, and that their thoughts and feelings are understandable. We don't have to agree with them, or like what they are doing, to give them this message. We are just affirming that their thoughts and feelings are understandable. Consider this interaction. A parent hears her child yelling at a friend and tries to find out what's going on.

Parent: What's going on? Why are you yelling?
Child: Nick's being mean! I don't like him.
Parent: You seem mad. What's going on?
Child: Nick won't play what I want to play.
Parent: Hm. Tell me more.
Child: He wants to play LEGOs, but I want to go play outside.
Parent: You're upset because Nick won't do what you want to do?
Child: Right.
Parent: It can be really frustrating when we don't get to do what we want, right? If you want to play together, you'll need to compromise and find something else to play or take turns. It is not OK to yell at your friends. It's not nice and hurts their feelings. Did you think that you might be hurting Nick's feelings? What can we do to help Nick feel better?

What happened in this interaction? What did the parent do that was validating? How did she communicate that she disagreed with her son? The parent acknowledged the child's feeling of frustration and conveyed an understanding of why the child was frustrated. At the same time, the parent communicated that yelling at a friend is not OK and that by asking what can be done to help the friend feel better, the parent is offering a way to repair the situation and relationship.

When we validate, we are also getting really valuable information about what is upsetting or affecting our child in a challenging or heated situation. When we listen actively, reflect, and connect, we are also providing ourselves with important guidance about what to do for our child. We want to do the right thing to help and to be effective. When we pair Wise Mind and Validation, we equip ourselves with the tools for being balanced (see Chapter 11).

The goal of getting your own emotions under control is to use your Wise Mind, Validation, and Scaffolding strategies more effectively in a heated or difficult situation. (We discuss Scaffolding in more detail in Chapter 11.) Here's how to do those things in a heated or difficult situation with your child:

- **Wise Mind.** Take a couple of deep, long breaths. As you breathe in, check your inner well of wisdom; check in with your intuition about what your child needs. Your child might need some space, or a hug, or an acknowledgment of what they are feeling. Breathe again and continue to listen to your Wise Mind.
- **Validation.** Show your child that you are listening. Ask your child to tell you what is going on or what the problem is. Say something like, "Tell me what is going on." or "Tell me what the problem is." Tone will be important here—you want to make sure that it is calm and even.
  - Listen quietly. Nod and lean in as you are listening. Make eye contact.
  - Reflect back what your child said and what your child is probably feeling. Make note of what you think is making your child feel that way and check to see if that is true.
  - Connect, saying something like, "It sounds like (or looks like) you're really mad. Are you mad because of . . . ?"

Take a moment to reflect on your own experiences of validation and how to use this with your children.

- Get a piece of paper and something to write with.
- Think about a time you felt validated—what did the person do that made you feel validated? How did it make you feel?
- Now think of a time that you could have validated your child—what could you have said or done to validate your child? What would validating your child look or sound like? How would that feel for your child?
- Use these ideas next time your child is having big or difficult emotions.

CONCLUSION

Building a positive, accepting, and warm relationship with our children lays a foundation of trust and enjoyment that promotes their positive development. It can help to soothe or calm children who have strong emotional reactions and build their own capacity for self-soothing and emotion regulation. It also is a necessary foundation for effectively using Scaffolding (Chapter 11) and consistent limit-setting (Chapter 12).

CHAPTER 11

BE BALANCED

One of the parenting skills parents can practice is to Be Balanced. You can also think of this as *Step In–Step Back* or *Scaffolding*. This means supporting, structuring, and guiding your child's play and work when needed and letting your child be independent and autonomous when they are doing fine without your help. Let's think about the term *scaffolding*. Think of the construction of a building. When construction workers are working on a building, they often have scaffolding and netting on the outside. They can stand on the scaffolding while they are building up the building. Then, as the building is complete and strong, the scaffolding can come down. That's where we get the idea of scaffolding. We step in and provide support when needed, but we step back and allow independence when our child is showing their strengths.

Sometimes parents step in to help with, or even take over, a child's activity or work because the child is not doing it quite right or the way that the parent would do it. Sometimes parents offer too many suggestions and directions, not giving the child a chance to problem-solve and figure it out themself. Other times, parents leave their children to their own devices to the extent that the child struggles, feels frustrated, and fails or gives up. Being overengaged or underengaged can both be problematic. What is most effective is finding a balance of providing guidance and structure while also allowing autonomy, independence, and problem solving. This is a very challenging skill for parents. It means balancing being helpful with letting your child be independent, and the hard part is knowing when to do each.

In this chapter, we provide some suggestions for being balanced with your child in challenging situations. Being balanced, or *Step In–Step Back*, as we refer to it, is a set of skills that can be mastered with practice, with specific recommendations for strategies that we provide in this chapter.

BREAK IT DOWN

Scaffolding is common in educational contexts when thinking about how to help children learn a new concept or topic. Parents can use some of the same tools when thinking about how to support their children in building skills for regulating their emotions or engaging in appropriate or desired behaviors. A helpful way of thinking about this is to use a coaching analogy, thinking about how a coach helps players build skills in a sport. Scaffolding includes breaking down tasks, slowing down to listen and collaborate, and providing visual reminders.

- **Break down challenging tasks or behaviors** into small steps or manageable chunks. Sometimes we forget how calming down when we're upset, solving a problem, or doing a chore like cleaning your room is actually quite complicated. These things involve lots of steps that are not always obvious when someone is learning to do it. Think about the challenge your child is facing in parts or steps, and list or name the steps.
- **Slow down to listen** to your child share how they were approaching the challenge, to understand what parts they are already

understanding and doing well and what parts need more structure and support. Talk about why this behavior or task is important to you and your child. Collaborate with your child in coming up with a plan, strategies, or steps for breaking down the parts that are harder.

- **Show how to do it, and then work side by side at first.** As your child gets the hang of it, you can start stepping back and letting them try on their own.
- **Think out loud,** sharing your own thinking and problem-solving processes when you are helping your child work through a challenging situation. Model noticing your feelings, assessing the situation, commenting on what is hard about the situation, thinking through your options, and then making a plan. Children gain more skills from watching and hearing how we cope with a tough problem than when we demonstrate our mastery and success with the problem.
- **Provide visual reminders.** These can be lists for the steps needed to complete the challenging task, or a prompt or code word that your child comes up with that can be taped to a mirror or door to remind them to use their strategies for calming down. For children who can't read, create an image or mini-comic strip with images that remind them what they are supposed to do.

OUR WAY OR THEIR WAY?

One aspect of being balanced is the need to reflect on whether it is important or necessary for our children to do things in a particular way versus accomplishing something in their own way. Sometimes we step in to tell our children how to do something, or even take over because they are not doing it the way we would do it. At times, that is necessary, but other times our children's own way of doing something or figuring out a problem can be effective even if it might not be as efficient or direct, or it might be just as good but different from our way. One of the harder things for parents in being balanced is not jumping in unnecessarily.

RESPONSIVE RESPONDING

In balancing providing guidance and structure with allowing autonomy, parents need to match their response to their children's needs. This requires being aware of our children's emotions and needs and then responding in a way that addresses those needs. We use our observing and noticing practices to recognize cues our children give us when they are starting to struggle with something. Cues can be in our children's facial expressions, body language, emotions, and words. We then match our responses to their needs, both in terms of what we do and how much we do it. Responses should be contingent and relevant. *Contingency* means that we offer our children the support or solution when they actually need it, in response to their cues, not randomly and not when we feel like it because of convenience or because certain responses make us feel good as parents. And *relevant* responses are those that actually address the child's need or emotion at the time. This is a challenging practice, and parents might not always get it right, which is OK. Practice being present, using the noticing and Wise Mind practices from Chapter 9. Check in with your child, noticing their verbal and nonverbal cues to assess whether what you did was responsive, and adjust as needed.

WISE MIND

One skill that helps us to be balanced and decide when to step in or step back is Wise Mind, which we discussed as part of being present in Chapter 9. Wise Mind is another way of being balanced, when we pause; hold both our emotional and rational reactions to a situation in mind; and find their balance, or the middle way to help us decide what is needed and what will be effective.

STEP IN–STEP BACK DURING CHILD-LED TIME

Child-Led Time (see Chapter 10) is a chance to practice Step In–Step Back. When you follow your child's lead, you let your child assert their desires or needs. Your child gets to decide what to play and how (as long as their behavior is appropriate and it is safe). Your job is just to follow and go with the flow. That is supporting autonomy or independence.

However, in Child-Led Time you can also notice if your child is getting off track in some way, struggling with something or not able to do it all by themself. There may be some time when your child is getting emotional, having problems settling into a fun activity, or engaging in behaviors that are inappropriate. These are just the times to think of stepping in to provide support. For example, if you're working on a puzzle, be engaged, but also let your child try pieces on their own. If your child is struggling for a few seconds, you can ask yourself, "What is needed? What will be effective?" and take a few more seconds to practice accessing your Wise Mind by dropping into the pauses or doing Wise Mind Breathing. If you decide your child could use some support or help, you can ask, "Can I try to help you with that?" and let your child decide if they are ready for help yet or would like to keep working on it. Or, if your child is trying to tell you something but can't quite get the words out right, you can first encourage them to keep trying, by saying, "Keep trying" or "Tell me more." You can try to help with thinking about a word they might need, without trying to say the whole idea or sentence they are trying to say. Then, if they still need help, you can take a stab at it and ask, "Is this what you mean . . .?"

The idea behind Step In–Step Back is that you can step in with structure and guidance at times when your child seems to struggle, stepping in just enough to help your child get back to a good place, where you and your child are calm and engaged. Here's where you put together your noticing skills and Wise Mind, and use those to step in as needed. So, you let your child be independent, and also provide support and guidance—but just enough so that your child can keep being independent.

Can you think of an example of a time when you supported your child in trying something independently? Can you think of a time when maybe you helped too much, or just took over doing something for your child because they were struggling? We all do it, so don't worry. We do that because we want the best for our children. We all want to be there to do what is needed. But let's think about what they learn from a situation when we help too much. Children learn fewer skills and gain less confidence when we do too much for them. They might become too dependent or don't learn to problem-solve when faced with a challenge. On the other hand, if they are allowed too much independence, and the task is over their head, they also don't learn any useful skills and they start to believe that they are helpless in difficult situations. You can see that it takes a delicate balance.

Parents often ask—how much help is too much? Or how much should I let my child struggle? Research shows that children learn best when they have the opportunity to be successful about 85% of the time and have the chance to struggle or fail 15% of the time (Blue, 2019). Thus, we want to step in to support success about 85% of the time, but we want to make sure they have a chance to try, struggle, and maybe fail about 15% of the time.

Here's a summary of how Step In–Step Back works:

- **Observe and notice.** You're noticing your child is getting off track. Your child is either getting frustrated or emotional, struggling with what they want to do—or your child's

behavior is getting out of control or inappropriate. Be Present to observe and notice your child's facial expression and body language.
- **Use your Active Listening.** Listen to what your child is saying and expressing. Reflect it back—say it back so your child knows that you heard them.
- **Check your Wise Mind.** Ask yourself, "What does my child need right now?" Take a few long breaths and check your Wise Mind as you breathe in. Ask yourself, "What will be effective for my child right now?"
- **Step in (as needed) and then step back (when your child is doing well).** Step in with your support and guidance, using your intuition for what your child might need. Say something like, "Can I try to help?" or "Can we try this to . . . ?" or "How about if we do this . . . ?" or "Maybe we can do this option or that option. What do you think?"

Our goal in using Step In–Step Back to manage and support our children's behaviors is to be effective, not necessarily right, and definitely not vindictive or punishing.

USING STEP IN–STEP BACK IN CHALLENGING SITUATIONS

Sometimes our children's behaviors may make us mad or frustrated, but our goal is to not take our frustration out on them or to be mad at them. Instead, our goal is to make the situation better, to be effective. When we can use Step In–Step Back with our children's challenging behaviors, we can be more effective in being clear about our expectations and encouraging children to do what is expected.

Sometimes parents are unclear about how to know when to step in and when to step back, worrying that they might make a mistake. Even if you make a mistake, it's still a good way to learn about your child's needs and to figure out what is needed and what will be effective in the future. Remember, we are practicing these skills, and we won't always get them right.

Parents also express concerns that when they step back they are not being supportive or loving. When a parent is being present and being warm, validating their child's experience and emotions, then stepping back can be the most effective way for the child to learn and therefore a way for parents to be supportive and loving.

One way to practice Step In—Step Back is to think about giving your child options for choosing a better way to do something. The Step In–Step Back worksheet in Exhibit 11.1 will help you think of ways to encourage and support acceptable and desirable behaviors to replace unacceptable behaviors.

Remember that we are talking about heated situations or problem behaviors. Usually, people in these interactions are upset, frustrated, angry, sad, or overwhelmed. In these emotionally charged situations, it's often hard to get the words out clearly and calmly. Instead, they often come out wrong.

With your Be Present skills, you can practice remaining calm. While you are doing that, you can also use Scaffolding skills to help your child communicate how they are feeling, guiding them in identifying their feelings and thoughts while doing so in an acceptable way. Here is where you balance structuring with autonomy support. Allowing autonomy means letting your child express their feelings and thoughts while you validate them. We don't want to punish our children or get them in trouble, or even discourage them for just saying what they think and feel. This involves the Validation skills we discussed in Chapter 10.

The guidance and structuring come in when you help your children label their feelings, clarify their thoughts, and help them

EXHIBIT 11.1. Step In–Step Back Worksheet

Think of a behavior your child engages in that you would like to change because it is unacceptable or undesirable:

For example, your child is jumping on the bed at bedtime when she or he is supposed to go to sleep.

Think of two options to suggest to your child that would be acceptable behaviors:

For example, let the child choose to read a book or sing a song with you while lying in bed.

1.

2.

Now, try it:

Use Step In–Step Back: Balance support for independence with just enough guidance and structure

1. Observe and notice. Notice your child is getting off track.
2. Active Listening. Listen to what your child is saying and expressing, and reflect it back.
3. Check your Wise Mind. Breathe and ask, "What is needed? What will be effective?"
4. Step In (as needed) and then Step Back (when child is doing well): Offer the two choices, and have your child choose one to replace what she or he is doing.

How did it work?

____

____

do those things in acceptable ways. Consider this interaction, which shows what we are talking about:

Child: Mom, can I go outside to play?

Mom: You can play outside after you pick up your toys in the family room.

Child: NOOOO, I want to play outside.

Mom: I understand you want to play outside. You can, after you clean up your mess.

Child: NOOOOO, you are sooo mean. I never get to do what I want.

Mom: [Using STOP—pausing to breathe, observe, and plan] I can tell that you are frustrated. I understand that you want to play, and you don't feel like cleaning up right now.

Child: I WANT TO GO OUTSIDE NOW.

Parent: Please say that calmly, like this: "Mom, I would like to go outside. I don't feel like cleaning up right now."

Child: Mom, I would like to go outside. I don't feel like cleaning up right now.

Mom: I understand that you want to go outside and you don't want to clean. And this is our rule, that you need to pick up your toys before you go out. Let's start together. The sooner it gets done, the sooner you can go out to play.

What skills or strategies do you see the mom using in that exchange? We know that it won't always go this way. We know there will be times when our child becomes oppositional, loses control, or we lose control. Let's resume this scenario but have it end differently:

Child: I WANT TO GO OUTSIDE NOW.
Mom: Please say that calmly, like this: "Mom, I would like to go outside. I don't feel like cleaning up right now."
Child: I WON'T!! You are being mean! [Throws a toy at mom.]

What do you think about that? How would a parent handle that? In Chapter 12, we offer some strategies for dealing with behaviors that are unacceptable or inappropriate.

You can practice Step In–Step Back. The worksheet in Exhibit 11.1 might be helpful as you practice. The more you practice this with your child, the more your child will get used to it and increasingly respond appropriately.

- Think of a behavior your child engages in that you would like to change because it is unacceptable or undesirable. For example, your child is jumping on the bed at bedtime when they are supposed to go to sleep.
- Now think of two options to suggest to your child that would be acceptable behaviors. For example, let the child choose to read a book or sing a song with you while lying in bed.
- Now try Step In–Step Back.
  - Observe and notice. Notice your child is getting off track.
  - Active Listening. Listen to what your child is saying and expressing, and reflect it back.
  - Check your Wise Mind. Breathe and ask, "What is needed? What will be effective?"
  - Step In (as needed) and then Step Back (when your child is doing well). Offer the two choices and have your child choose one to replace what they are doing.

How did it work? What can you adjust if it didn't work well?

CONCLUSION

Balancing guidance and structuring with giving your child autonomy and independence may be one of the more challenging parenting practices. We want to support our children to the extent that they are successful most of the time but also allow them to struggle a little to solve problems on their own. Parents can break down complicated tasks and support children through the steps of completing the task. We also need to pause and reflect on whether we are expecting our children to do things our way or if we're OK with them doing it their way. We can break down tasks and provide support in the areas where our children are struggling, and we can celebrate when they figure out how to do things on their own and in their own way.

CHAPTER 12

BE CONSISTENT

When we talk about being *consistent*, we are referring to creating predictability and order in a child's home life. It involves a parent being there consistently for their child as well as having consistent expectations for and responses to children's behaviors. It means being predictable in what you expect and how you enforce your expectations. This consistency in parents' expectations and responses to their children's behaviors helps to increase the things we want to see more of from our children and decrease the things we want to see less. Consistency is not only about increasing and decreasing behaviors, though. It's about providing children with an understandable environment that builds trusting relationships and cultivates self-regulation and autonomy. In this chapter, we explain how to be consistent with your expectations and responses.

HOW REINFORCEMENT AND CONSEQUENCES CHANGE BEHAVIOR

Most of the practices we describe in this chapter stem from an understanding of how reinforcement and consequences change behaviors in everyone. We all change our behavior as a function of what follows.

If the outcomes or consequences are good, we are more likely to do that same behavior again, and if they are not, then not so much. So, it follows that changing behavior, either increasing or decreasing its frequency (or probability of occurrence) can be accomplished by altering the consequences that follow. When desirable outcomes follow a given behavior, or set of behaviors, and when they follow close in time, these become linked, making that preceding behavior more likely to occur again, especially in a similar context. Consequences have to follow the behavior closely in time to cause a change, and effects of consequences will be more powerful in situations that are similar. For example, if you offer rewards (verbal or tangible) for following your directions at mealtime, your child will be more likely to cooperate around meals, more so than in other contexts. This learning principle holds true for everyone and is the basis of most of our efforts to change something we are doing, like increasing exercise or a new hobby or decreasing TV time or a bad habit. So, if I want to increase the likelihood that my child helps out around the house, noticing them doing so and providing a positive consequence (praise, opportunity to play a game) would be an effective approach. Maybe I want my child to start making dinner occasionally, but all they have done so far is bake desserts. I could start by asking that they help with one element, like a side dish or salad, or help prep part of the main dish, baby-stepping to more responsibility.

Negative consequences can be effective, yet we have found in our work with families clinically, and in our personal experiences as parents, that establishing a home routine with ample positive reinforcement opportunities provides a foundation for the ability to remove these reinforcers, in effect creating negative consequences without introducing something aversive like a punishment. Of course, really serious transgressions—for example, behaviors with potentially dangerous outcomes—will likely require removal of reinforcement and a negative consequence.

What are *reinforcers*? They are positive consequences that are perceived as positive and, importantly, function to increase the frequency of the behavior they are intended to reinforce. Circular, we know . . . a reinforcer is anything your child is interested in and willing to work for, ranging from stickers to selecting games, movies, and an opportunity to choose a snack or a meal, to name a few.

Sometimes parents think that setting up a system wherein such reinforcers can be earned amounts to bribery, but we beg to differ. Bribes are given in an effort to get someone (e.g., a politician) to violate a law, rule, or regulation—to do something wrong or inappropriate. Reinforcers are meant to encourage positive, correct behaviors that are, in fact, appropriate. Think of providing reinforcement as facilitating learning, which is how it is framed in the science of psychology—reinforcement is a primary topic in courses that address learning. Sometimes parents also think that using reinforcers and consequences is manipulative or an effort to control our children rather than teach and nurture them. This can be true when these are not used correctly, and in this chapter we offer suggestions for being thoughtful and effective. But it is important to recognize that reinforcers and consequences are an inherent part of almost every experience and a natural process for increasing or decreasing behaviors. For example, if you get together with a friend and you don't enjoy the time at all because the person talked about themselves the whole time and didn't ask you anything about yourself, you are much less likely to spend time with this person in the future because it was a negative experience and not reinforcing. Another example might come from your work setting. You get paid to do your job. You most likely wouldn't do the work if you weren't paid. The pay is your reinforcer. If you do a great job or put in extra effort at work, you might get a pay raise, which reinforces doing a great job. If you don't do a particularly good job, you probably won't get a raise and might even get fired. Those are negative consequences that might decrease the likelihood that you would do that again. These examples show how reinforcers and consequences are present throughout our lives. It is not unnatural, manipulative, or controlling to build them into our children's lives.

Being consistent in facilitating learning through reinforcement is important, especially when we are just starting the process or are working to shape the behavior—starting with something similar to what we want (making desserts) and progressing toward what we actually want (making dinner). Consistency is also really critical for children who get frustrated easily, are impulsive, and are fearless.

Parents might have heard that providing reinforcement or rewards for behaviors reduces children's internal or natural motivation to engage in those behaviors. This is true for things that our kids love to do inherently. If your child loves reading and is highly motivated to read on their own, and you start offering rewards for reading, your child's intrinsic motivation for reading will decline over time. So, if your child is intrinsically motivated to read, do their homework diligently, help cook dinner, clean their room, or help with chores, you can just enjoy working with them. There is no need to create reinforcements for those behaviors. But if parents want to increase their children's engagement in activities or behaviors that they are not naturally and internally motivated to engage in, creating rewarding or reinforcing outcomes or consequences for those activities is recommended.

The following strategies are all ways to think about incorporating reinforcers and consequences into your parenting in effective ways. We then include some tips for specific situations, such as managing bedtimes, homework, chores, and so on, in Chapter 13.

NOTICE THE GOOD

One effective reinforcer is noticing and commenting on when your child is doing what you expect. Many times, we call out their misbehaviors or failure to meet expectations, but we can also notice and praise when they are doing well. This helps your child recognize and persist in appropriate behaviors you value and encourage. You can practice noticing and commenting on their positive behaviors throughout the day—for example, when they are focused and working on their homework, or when they pick up a room without being asked, or when they sit and chat with you while you're preparing dinner. You can express appreciation and enjoyment of those times.

HAVE CLEAR EXPECTATIONS AND CONTINGENCIES

There will be times when our children are out of control emotionally or engaging in unacceptable behaviors. When we think about managing our children's challenging behaviors or misbehaviors, we can think about it in the context of using Wise Mind and Scaffolding. Our goal in managing our children's problem behaviors is to be effective, not necessarily right, and definitely not vindictive or punishing. Their behaviors may make us mad or frustrated, but our goal is to not take our frustration out on them or to be mad at them. Our emotions are valid, and at the same time our goal is to make the situation better. That means that our goal is not to punish our child or prove that we are right but to effectively change our child's behavior to be more appropriate or desirable. We can do that by scaffolding the situation and by being consistent. When children are engaging in undesirable or inappropriate behaviors, we can think about providing the following:

- **Clear guidance or guidelines.** Let them know clearly what behavior is expected or appropriate.
- **Options for engaging in appropriate behavior.** Give them a couple of choices for correcting their behavior and for meeting your expectations. Letting them choose an appropriate behavior supports their autonomy, which builds self-regulation.
- **Consistent contingencies.** Have a plan that reinforces (rewards) children with attention and privileges when they meet our

expectations (e.g., noticing when they are doing what we expect) and having consequences or losing privileges when they break rules or engage in unacceptable behaviors.

To do these, we have to have clear expectations, our children have to know our expectations, and we use privileges and consequences when children do or don't do what we expect. We are all subject to similar patterns of rewards and negative consequences. Think about your own relationships or work. If you do things well or interact appropriately with people, meeting their expectations, there are natural rewards for that: positive outcomes. If you make mistakes or don't act the way you are supposed to, violating expectations, there are natural consequences: negative outcomes. Those are the contingencies of our actions.

By letting our children know what we expect, we are providing the guidance and structuring they need, and by giving them options for meeting our expectations we are giving them the independence to make choices and have some freedom. This is both scaffolding your child's behavior and being consistent.

When you are scaffolding children's behaviors, keep those three list items (clear guidelines or expectations, options for appropriate behaviors, and contingencies for meeting or not meeting those expectations) in mind. For example, if your child is about to write on a book with a marker, you can say, "This book is for reading, and we want to take care of our books that we read. That marker will ruin the book, and we want to take care of the things in our house." That part tells your child that your expectation is that they will respect the property in your house. "You can write on this paper with the marker, or you can get your coloring book and color in there. Which do you want to do?" This part lets your child know that there are other options that allow them to use the marker in a way that IS acceptable. Providing guidance and structure for our children includes structuring the contingencies or consequences of their actions.

REWARDS AND CONSEQUENCES

This is a good place to take a minute to practice defining an expectation, privilege, and consequence that we can work on with our children. What comes to mind as the most critical expectation for your child, and what are the ways that your child can meet that expectation or expectations? What is the behavior you want your child to do more of? Less of?

In our work with families experiencing clinically significant challenges with their children's behavior, it became clear that picking broader, gatekeeping behaviors is most effective. For example, you may wish that your child didn't fight with siblings, took the dog for a walk when asked, or turned to homework immediately after school (before video games, etc.). All of these behaviors have something in common—they are all examples of a lack of, or limited, cooperation in their present form. Your child may not cooperate after being told multiple times to share, or to use their indoor voice when talking to siblings, or they may instigate a fight over whose turn it is to play a particular game. If you have communicated a rule or boundary indicating that certain behaviors represent the norm, such as "You have to ask your brother nicely," you can expect compliance around this norm, reinforcing it when it occurs. Note that the rule or direction being provided in this example is, in essence, the opposite of the behavior we want to decrease—that is, fighting with a sibling. This is really important because we can be far more effective increasing, as opposed to decreasing, a behavior. From the standpoint of learning principles, a child will learn more efficiently when they are told what to do, as opposed to what not to do, which is a much broader category and does not actually point to the desired behavior in a meaningful way. Rewarding your child for different examples of compliance teaches them how to generalize this cooperative attitude across tasks and situations.

An additional caveat is warranted insofar as no child is cooperative 100% of the time, and this is not the goal. However, when children fall below about 75% rate of compliance, this becomes noticeable to adults, who are typically annoyed and irritated as their instructions are often not followed as expected.

SCAFFOLDING OR CONSEQUENCES?

Basically, we want to reinforce or reward acceptable behaviors, and we want to have negative consequences for unacceptable behaviors. In heated or emotionally charged situations, we are much more likely to see behaviors as unacceptable, even when they might not be. It will be very important to remember what is an acceptable expression of a charged or heated emotion versus what is an unacceptable behavior.

Let's think about this—which of the behaviors in Table 12.1 do you think are unacceptable and require a consequence? Some of these may not be so clear. Any of these child reactions are possible and more likely when we are in a heated, angry exchange. At those times, we as parents aren't always at our best either. In the middle of all of that, we can get heated or emotionally charged ourselves. We are less likely to think clearly, and it is harder to keep our own cool.

It is at these times, more than ever, that we will need to have practiced our STOP and Parent Time Out skills ahead of time (see Chapter 9). And it is at these times that we will need to use our preplanned consequences for inappropriate behaviors. These are things like using Time Out From Positive Reinforcement (which we discuss in more detail later in this chapter) or removing a privilege. But when we are angry or aroused, and not thinking clearly, we are more likely

TABLE 12.1. Responding to Your Child's Behavior

Behavior	Appropriate response
Is your child emotional, crying, or upset?	Validate, soothe, and scaffold
Is your child yelling at you?	Scaffold instead of giving consequences
Is your child telling you they are mad at you?	Can be acceptable
Is your child calling you a name?	Scaffold or consequence. If there is a rule about name-calling, this might require a consequence.
Is your child cursing?	If there is a rule about no cursing, then this is something that should receive a consequence.
Is your child slamming a door?	Scaffold instead of consequence.
Is your child throwing something soft, like a pillow or towel?	Scaffold instead of consequence.
Is your child throwing something hard, but not at anyone?	Scaffold or consequence, or both
Is your child throwing something hard at someone?	Consequence
Is your child hitting something like a pillow or their bed?	Can be acceptable
Is your child hitting a wall?	Scaffold instead of consequence
Is your child hitting a person?	Consequence
What are some examples in your family?	How do you respond?

to say and do things that are aimed at making our child feel bad, or making them really sorry for what they did by making the consequence really severe or piling on consequences. These are often then taken back because, for example, it is likely not reasonable to ground a child for a month or take away their TV/media privileges for that long. Sometimes we may blurt out consequences that inadvertently punish the entire family, such as: "I guess we can't go to Grandma's because you are not able to respect others and keep your hands to yourself." Here is where we are really tested. The best way to get through these challenging times is to be ready with potential consequences and perhaps even a script of what you could say in the event a consequence becomes necessary.

We can also be ready when we have practiced using our Be Present skills regularly and when we have gotten into a routine of using a behavior management plan. This plan will likely include the use of Time Out From Positive Reinforcement because we need tools to extinguish inappropriate behaviors, along with those that encourage appropriate ones. We talk more about using Time Out later in this chapter.

BEHAVIOR MANAGEMENT PLAN

When you consider the expectations and rules in your family, you will take into account your families' values and interests. Every family will identify their own "behavioral targets"—behaviors in your child that you want to encourage or reward, which we can accomplish by noticing and paying attention to those behaviors and reinforcing them with privileges and rewards. You can also identify behaviors that you might want to decrease or that are unacceptable in your family, and you can do that by having negative consequences for undesirable or inappropriate behaviors.

When we are consistent with our children, when we are clear and consistent about our expectations and provide consistent reinforcement and consequences, we build trust and predictability in our relationship with our children, and we build predictability and stability in our children's lives. These are critical for building our children's social–emotional well-being and self-regulation. Use the "Be Consistent" worksheet in Exhibit 12.1 to help make a plan for behaviors that you would like to address with your child. You can also use the Behavior Management Plan Log in Exhibit 12.2 to track your progress and note what did or did not work well.

MORE ABOUT CONTINGENCIES

Managing contingencies requires the steps we've already discussed: (a) identify desirable and undesirable behaviors, (b) set clear expectations about what to do, (c) clearly establish and communicate what are desirable and undesirable behaviors, and (d) set reasonable limits using appropriate contingency management (positive reinforcement and negative consequences). Sometimes there are natural consequences, and we do not have to step in with any additional removal of privileges. For example, if your child's play date ends early because they were not able to share or were making their friend only play by their rules, this is already a powerful consequence, which you can increase in effectiveness. After empathizing with the situation and validating your child's feelings of disappointment over a lost opportunity to play, it is possible to point out that sharing and changing up who gets to decide how to play will make the situation more enjoyable for a friend next time. You can then have your child practice offering toys and asking a friend to take a turn setting up rules before the next play encounter.

EXHIBIT 12.1. Be Consistent: Developing a Behavior Management Plan

1. Provide clear guidance or guidelines—let your child know what is expected or appropriate.
2. Provide options for engaging in appropriate behavior—give your child options for correcting the misbehavior and for meeting expectations.
3. Consistent contingencies—have a plan for privileges for expected behaviors and consequences for breaking rules or misbehaving.

When we have clear expectations and rules for our children, their lives are more predictable, and we can be more effective in helping them meet those expectations.

List a family value or expectation you have for your child. Clarify what is acceptable and unacceptable: (e.g., Be Respectful—we expect you to be gentle and to speak respectfully. Or Help Around the House—we expect you to pick up after yourself and help with some chores.)

•
•

List two specific things your child is expected to do to meet that value. These are "target behaviors" to work on. Name one thing your child should do more (increase) and one you would like them to do less (decrease): for example, "Say please," "No hitting," or "Pick up your toys from the house," "Don't throw your laundry on the floor in your room".

- Target 1—Increase:
- Target 2—Decrease:

List what you expect of your child in this area:

- Target 1 Expectation:
- Target 2 Expectation:

Check if your expectations are developmentally appropriate. Is your child old enough to be able to do this?

EXHIBIT 12.1. Be Consistent: Developing a Behavior Management Plan (*Continued*)

List a privilege or reward that is associated with doing the target would like to increase. What does your child get or get to do when s/he meets your expectations?

- Privilege or reward to increase Target 1:

List a consequence that is associated with the target you would like to decrease. What will happen when your child doesn't do what s/he is expected to?

- Consequence to decrease Target 2:

Explain your expectations to your children. Explain that there will be a privilege or reward when they meet Target 1, and there will be a consequence when they do the thing you don't want, Target 2. Let your child know what the reward and consequence will be.

EXHIBIT 12.2. Behavior Management Plan Log

Date	Talked with child about target	Child did it? Yes/No	Consequence?	Privilege/ reward?

PRECISE DIRECTIONS

Another relevant skill set has to do with relying on what we refer to as *Precise Directions*.[1] These are what they sound like: precisely worded and clear directions. Stating what you mean as precisely as possible in moments when you are attempting to get your child to cooperate with instructions maximizes success. These directions are concise, using as few words as possible, avoiding lectures and explanations. We are certainly not suggesting that you talk to your child like a drill sergeant, yet it is important to indicate in your wording and tone that you mean what you say—that this is not a request that can be contemplated or ignored. Also, it's important to form these instructions around what to do (rather than what not to do), in order to avoid any confusion. Being told what not to do leaves a lot of room for interpretation of what would actually be acceptable. This means that if you are focusing on undesirable behavior you will need to come up with its opposite (e.g., "Use gentle hands" instead of "Stop being rough"), or some alternative behavior that can be put in its place (maybe "Clean up before dinner" instead of "Stop arguing with your brother"). Here are some additional related recommendations:

- **Statement format.** Say, "it is time to . . .," "Please sit down," and so on. Do not use questions or a "Let's" format, such as "Why don't you . . .?" or "Let's sit down, OK?"
- **"Start" requests.** Tell the child what you want them to start doing rather than what you want them to stop doing.
- **Time.** Wait 3 to 5 seconds after making a request. Do not talk to the child or engage in any other activity during this time.

---

[1]The following exercise, Precise Directions, is adapted from one created by R. J. McMahon and R. L. Forehand.

- **Give a command or request only twice.** After waiting an initial 3 to 5 seconds for the child to comply, repeat the request. Consequences must be applied if the child does not comply after being asked twice. It helps to have a key word, such as "need" or "now," in the second request, which cues the child that this is their last chance to comply before earning the negative consequence.
- **Distance.** Get within 3 feet of the child before giving the command or request.
- **Eye contact.** Establish eye contact before making the request.
- **Touching.** It may help to lightly touch the child on the arm or shoulder before making the request. Do not do this if the child is older or prefers not to be touched.
- **Voice tone.** A firm, but soft tone of voice works best.
- **Remain nonemotional.** Making threats or becoming angry will decrease your effectiveness.
- **Be specific.** Describe in specific terms what you want the child to do. Instead of saying, "It's time to get back to work" say, "It's time to finish this math worksheet."
- **Positive consequences.** Praise the child every time they comply with a request. Try to vary the praise statements you use, because this will sound more genuine, and be as specific in your praise as possible—"I like how you started your homework when I reminded you it was time" is better than "Good job."
- **Negative consequences.** Do not threaten. Preplanned (mild) consequences must be applied whenever the child does not comply after the second request. Consistent follow-through is essential to making this work.

Precise directions are not about being a drill sergeant, but they do require planning and firmness. Instructions should be concise and descriptive and are most effective when you are telling your impulsive child what to do, *not* what not to do—remember, they have a hard time putting the brakes on. Do not yell at them from another room! First of all, yelling reflects negative emotions (i.e., anger and frustration). Second, you have not gotten their attention, which you can ensure only with physical proximity and eye contact, maybe even touching. Firmness comes into play with not endlessly repeating the same instructions but stopping after a second command. Negative consequences do not have to be extensive. In fact, *mild* means brief and not particularly aversive (e.g., losing some screen time or another desired activity for a period of time). Be careful not to indicate consequences that are too severe to be carried out ("You are grounded for a month!") or those that will affect others in the family ("No TV tonight!"). We often tell parents to practice what they are going to say and how they are going to say it. Power struggles can easily ensue and are typically stressful, thus requiring a certain level of preparedness in terms of strategies and responses at one's fingertips. The more prepared you are, the more effective precise directions will be.

TIME IN AND TIME OUT: ATTENTION AS REINFORCEMENT

We want to talk in detail about a very powerful tool for supporting your child's self-regulation and for managing misbehaviors. That tool is ATTENTION—specifically, your attention. What your child treasures more than anything is when you pay attention to them, and this can be used strategically to increase behaviors you want to see more of. On the other hand, withdrawing attention or ignoring can be used to decrease behaviors we want to see less of. This requires that we think about Time Out in a very different way than most people think about it or use it. We are going to talk about two things: Time Out From Attention and Time Out From Positive Reinforcement.[2] When

[2]The following exercise, Precise Directions, is adapted from one created by R. J. McMahon and R. L. Forehand.

we talk about *Time Out From Attention*, we are referring to ignoring or not paying attention to minor misbehaviors or undesirable behaviors, while other forms of reinforcement (e.g., enjoyable activities) are still available. When we refer to *Time Out From Positive Reinforcement*, we are talking about applying a formal Time Out—this is what most people think of when they hear the term "Time Out," and it involves the withdrawal not only of your attention but also of all other sources of reinforcement or rewarding activities.

Both forms of Time Out (Time Out From Attention and Time Out From Positive Reinforcement) can be very effective in changing our children's behaviors, given that there is ample Time In. But Time Outs—that is, what most people think of as a Time Out—are often used or done incorrectly, and we now discuss using Time In and Time Out effectively. When children misbehave, it is important that parents have a clear plan for how to address the misbehavior in a way that teaches the child what is expected and decreases the chances that a misbehavior happens again. Often, not attending is sufficient in reducing minor annoying behaviors, such as whining or complaining, but at other times behaviors we want to reduce or discourage are more significant, like hitting or kicking, or may be dangerous, so another course of action is required.

Let's take just a moment to talk about how both types of Time Out work—this provides important context for why we approach time out in the way that we do. First of all, there's no such thing as Time Out without Time In. *Time In* refers to giving your child your time and attention. It means that your child enjoys their time with you, wants to be with you, and feels warmth and a connection from their relationship with you. Warmth and responsiveness have to come first, and when your child is experiencing positive attention from you they will be motivated to change their behavior to have more of it. Take a look at Table 12.2 as we explain how attention Time In and Time Out work to increase and decrease behaviors.

TABLE 12.2. Time In From Attention or Positive Reinforcement Versus Time Out From Attention or Positive Reinforcement

Time In or Time Out?	Child OK behavior	Child not-OK behavior
Time In From Attention or Positive Reinforcement	(↑)	↑
Time Out From Attention or Positive Reinforcement	↓	(↓)

Time In Increases Behaviors

Giving our attention to our children increases our warm, positive relationship with them. Children want our attention, and it is a huge driving force for their behavior. Children seek attention, whether it's positive attention OR negative attention. We call this the "attention rule," which basically is: Children want it. In a Time In situation, this means that you are acting interested in what the child is doing, talking with them, playing with them, and expressing that you are enjoying your time with them. This type of Time In really encourages behaviors we have identified as acceptable or desirable. This is what Child-Led Time (see Chapter 10) is for.

When our child is trying to get our attention, we might see an increase in unacceptable behaviors. Remember, our kids want our attention, whether it's positive or negative. So, if they can't get our attention in a positive way they will be satisfied with getting our attention in a negative way—when we are getting after them or yelling at them for something they've done wrong, or trying to have a discussion about their misbehaviors. That kind of attention actually leads to an INCREASE in unacceptable behavior, *especially if it's the only attention they get from us*. Attention can reinforce unacceptable behavior.

Attention may take the form of talking or engaging with your child, maybe explaining what they did wrong or trying to convince them to stay in a Time Out From Positive Reinforcement location. You may be giving them attention for a tantrum that they are throwing or negotiating with them about why they are in Time Out From Positive Reinforcement. Lots of parents do this because it is really tempting to talk with your child in this way. But one thing we can probably all agree—it's really hard to talk your child into being good!

Time Out From Attention Decreases Behaviors

If we want to decrease unacceptable behaviors, we have to spend less time paying attention to those behaviors. That's where ignoring small unacceptable or annoying behaviors and using a formal Time Out for more serious behaviors comes in. We want to remove our attention and other reinforcements to reduce unacceptable behaviors. On the other hand, we might not be giving our children our attention when we should be. It's really easy to miss the times they are doing what we expect them to. When they are playing quietly or independently, or playing nicely with their siblings or friends, we tend to miss it or ignore it because it gives us some time to do what we need to do. We might be spending a lot of time on the phone, or on a computer, or doing other things, and not noticing their good behavior or not giving them some of our attention a little bit every day. Sometimes, catching our children being good means attending to them when they are being neutral. Maybe your older child is not excited about being stuck in the car's backseat with a younger sibling and friends, but they are not complaining or whining about it. This is probably a good time to note that you appreciate them being a good sport about this arrangement. When our children are not getting attention, reinforcement, and warmth when they are engaging in desirable behaviors, this could lead to decreases in acceptable behaviors or increases in unacceptable behaviors.

We know that we can't pay attention to our children all the time, which is why setting aside time when they can get your undivided attention, or Child-Led Time, is so important. It's a way that we can give our children some positive attention every day. Our children want our attention, but if we don't give it to them regularly then we see a decrease in acceptable behaviors.

Let's look at Exhibit 12.2 again. When we use Time In to build a positive, warm relationship with our child and catch them being good, noticing their desirable behaviors, Time Out From Attention and Time Out From Positive Reinforcement are more effective because they remove the reinforcement of our attention. In this situation, your child will work hard to stay out of Time Out From Positive Reinforcement and maintain your attention. That's what we want! They are mostly getting your attention during Time In—and they want that attention more than almost anything.

So, if you have very little Time In when your child is engaging in acceptable behaviors, then Time Out, both ignoring and official Time Outs, won't really work for you. And if you give a lot of attention during an official Time Out, then it will also not work. Also, overreliance on giving Time Outs will dampen their effectiveness. Time Out works best when you have Time Ins—you give attention—regularly, and when you remove attention when there is misbehavior and use Time Out From Positive Reinforcement sparingly (choosing ignoring for more minor transgressions instead).

Time Out From Positive Reinforcement

Let's talk about Time Out From Positive Reinforcement in more detail. As noted, applying a Time Out From Positive Reinforcement is something we would consider using for more serious misbehavior, not for little annoying behaviors or when you disagree with your child. For those, ignoring or removing attention is recommended. An official Time Out is used when your child misbehaves or doesn't comply with a parent directive. What a family considers a serious behavior is up to each family. But these would be things like hitting a sibling during an argument, throwing something at someone, or some other destructive behavior. How to implement Time Out From Positive Reinforcement most effectively for these more problematic behaviors will also vary depending on the family context, yet some general guidelines can be offered.

Remember that we want a Time Out From Positive Reinforcement to be a situation that doesn't include a lot of your attention or other reinforcement or reward for your child. As a general rule of thumb, it's best for Time Out places to be boring, free from distractions, well lit, and well ventilated. It's usually a good idea to avoid the bathroom and the child's own room. Many parents use a chair that is in the corner of a family room or kitchen, or the bottom stair of a flight of stairs (note, for safety reasons it's very important this is the bottom step).

In general, Time Out From Positive Reinforcement works best for one of two situations: either when your child has broken a significant rule in your home (e.g., hitting or name-calling a sibling or being unsafe) or when your child has decided to not comply with a direction you have given them. There are different ideas about how long to have a child in Time Out, but a good rule of thumb is about 1 minute for every year of age. If your child has a really hard time paying attention and sitting still, you can shorten the time out to maybe 2 minutes total (it will FEEL like 3–4 minutes for this type of child!). The idea is that it should be long enough so that your child calms down but not so long that it becomes overly punishing.

You, as the parent, are the one who decides how long the Time Out should be and when your child can get out of Time Out. Although it's tempting to let a child out of Time Out "when they feel like they are ready" to be out of Time Out, it is important that you, as the parent, stay in control of how long the Time Out will last. It is also really important that your child is calm when they get out of Time Out. For this reason, we recommend that your child stay in Time Out for the entire time and that, in order to get out of Time Out, they are quiet and calm for at least 15 seconds. If this happens during the normal Time Out period, then that's great, and you can let your child out right away when their time is up. If your child is still upset at the end of their Time Out, then Time Out should simply continue until you get those 15 seconds of quiet.

For a situation when a child has broken a rule and/or is doing something that puts themselves or someone else in the family at risk for getting hurt, you would tell your child exactly what they did wrong and place them immediately in Time Out for the designated time. It's often a good idea to set a timer. Remember, after you tell your child why they are going to Time Out and put them in their quiet place, you should not give them any more attention, even if they're saying they are sorry or that they won't do it again. So, if a child breaks a rule, do the following:

1. Tell the child that they broke the rule and that the consequence is that they are going to Time Out.
2. Lead a child to Time Out, saying: "You are in Time Out for 3 minutes. I will come get you when your Time Out is over."
3. Once Time Out is over, remind the child of the rule. It is very important that you don't hold a grudge. When the Time Out is over, resume normal interactions, showing warmth and responsiveness.

After a Time Out, it is very important that parents engage in Time In, that is, re-engaging attention. Remember, Time Out only works when there is ample Time In.

DIRECTIVE FOLLOW-THROUGH

The other situation when Time Out is particularly helpful is when your child is not following your instruction. We have a couple of tips for this. First, you want your instruction to be as clear as possible (i.e., a Precise Direction). We don't want to give a child a Time Out just because they didn't understand what was being requested of them. Some common traps for unclear instructions include vague instructions; instructions worded as questions; too many instructions at one time; too much detail about a request; and "Let's" commands (e.g., "Let's clean up"), where the child thinks that perhaps you and they are going to be doing the task together when your intention is for them to do it themselves. We all give these types of instructions from time to time. We just want to watch for how often they happen and be mindful of trying to be as clear as possible, using Precise Directions as much as possible.

The second tip is to give your child about 5 seconds to comply. When giving an instruction, in a way you are asking a child to stop doing something they are engaged in and to start doing something else. For little children, it sometimes takes a little bit of time for them to really process what you are requesting of them. These 5 seconds allow for your child to redirect their attention and give you an opportunity to reflect on the pathway and perhaps prepare yourself in case you will need to use Time Out. Many parents find that this is a perfect time to practice some deep breathing (or +2 Breathing) so that they can enter into the Time Out situation calm and with a feeling that they are in control. So, in this situation you provide an instruction and wait 5 seconds. Then, one of two things happens: Either your child complies, or they do not. If they comply, what should we do? Shower them with praise noting their cooperation (i.e., offering descriptive praise: "I like how you were able to turn to your homework when I told you to do so") and that it is appreciated.

If they don't comply, then we would repeat the instruction, this time reminding them that if they don't comply they will get a Time Out or other prespecified consequence. Wait 5 seconds after repeating the instruction, with a reminder that if they do not follow through they will receive a Time Out or other consequence. Again, one of two things might happen. If your child follows through with the instruction this second time, then we would praise them for making a good choice and thank them for following through. Remember, we want to give our child about 5 seconds to make their decision. Finally, we may have a situation in which, despite being asked twice, your child does not comply. In this case, they would go to Time Out (or other prespecified consequence), following the same strategy for Time Out that we have discussed.

Here's the REALLY important thing: After a Time Out or the consequence is applied, it's critical that you repeat your original instruction. You should go through this sequence as many times as it takes until your child follows through with your instruction. Otherwise, what might your child learn? That's right, that they can choose between following your instruction and doing Time Out or getting a consequence. Remember to give specific praise when your child complies, such as "I appreciate that you did what I asked." You can use the "Practicing Time Out" worksheet in Exhibit 12.3 to track your progress.

We would like to address some parents' concerns about using Time Out From Positive Reinforcement. Some popular press reports have suggested that the use of Time Out can be damaging to a child's attachment security, especially for children who have

EXHIBIT 12.3. Practicing Time Out From Positive Reinforcement

List two rules in your family that would require a Time Out if your child broke the rule:

1.

2.

Date	What did your child do to break a rule?	How did you do Time Out?	What did your child do during Time Out?	What happened after Time Out?

Also, note two times this week that you gave your child an instruction. Write down what you asked your child to do, whether your child did it, and what you did in response (Specific praise? Time out? Forgot to notice? Other?).

Date	What did you ask your child to do?	Did your child do what you asked?	What did you do?	What happened after?

experienced trauma or adversity. There have even been some who claim Time Out is abusive. Time Out could be harmful when implemented incorrectly, for example, in a punitive or demeaning manner. However, we have shared an approach to Time Out that implements learning and self-regulation principles, and in a way that allows both the parent and child to calm down. When used in this way, it is consistently shown to be effective in reducing behavior problems and improving self-regulation and is not emotionally damaging (Dadds & Tully, 2019).

CONCLUSION

Understanding the principles of learning and behavioral reinforcement can help parents navigate their children's challenging behaviors, especially when they understand these in the context of the child's temperament. We have conveyed why it is important to be consistent, communicating clearly about family values, expectations, and rules and being consistent about following through with both reinforcement, praise or rewards for meeting those expectations, and negative consequences for not. You may have to try the different options presented here to determine what works for your child and your family. We should also note that attaining 100% consistency is not a feasible goal, nor is it necessary. Your child needs to experience consistency as a "critical mass" of your approach, and it's a good idea to have an explanation for deviation from the routine (e.g., no Time Outs at Grandma's house). It might be helpful to keep a log of the things you've tried and how they worked. (The worksheet in Exhibit 12.3 can help with this.) This can also help you track how consistently you are enacting the plans they have developed and make note of what works best with your child.

CHAPTER 13

BEING CONSISTENT WITH COMMON CHALLENGES

Parents often experience challenges in some key situations, including bedtime, mealtime, and homework routines; getting out the door in time for work or school; and getting their children to help with chores. The tools for being consistent that we discussed in Chapter 12 are particularly useful for navigating challenges commonly faced by parents. Parents can approach these challenges with an understanding of *contingency management*, that is, considering how to use reinforcements and consequences, as well as other tools for increasing desired behaviors. These will often lead to an increase in the preferred behavior and a decrease in the stress and distress that can arise in these situations.

BEDTIME ROUTINES

When I (Masha) was working with children and families in private practice, questions related to bedtime were very common, for children and adolescents of different ages. The nature of bedtime struggles changes with age, but some challenges can be present across the age spectrum.

Let's talk about babies first. Needless to say, babies come out of the womb not recognizing that we have all agreed to be awake and active during the day and sleep through the night. Most babies take a couple of months or so to get the whole day–night thing figured out, and of course they nap frequently during the day and wake up to have something to eat at night. As babies grow, and their need for steady nutrition decreases, it becomes physiologically possible for them to sleep through the night. However, a number continue to get their parents to provide nighttime feedings, likely because they appreciate the interaction, which they experience as reinforcing. In other words, parents providing attention, affection, and nutrition after infants awaken and cry for them in fact promotes the exact behavioral pattern that most parents will likely want to interrupt as the babies approach the end of the first year of life. We should also note that all children awaken at night at times, and the "good sleepers" are able to go back to sleep without parental intervention. It is important to recognize that families will make different choices about handling their infants' sleep, and these can be based on cultural or family values or needs. It is important that parents receive no judgment for their choices, either to respond to their babies at night or to let them establish the ability to go back to sleep without parental intervention. The important point here is to understand the reinforcing role that parental attention during the night can play. If a family is ready to reduce night awakenings, the behavioral principles we discuss in this chapter can help.

Another caveat is that if families have infants sleeping in their own beds, practicing separate sleeping arrangements and managing sleep problems in infancy is strongly recommended. As separately sleeping children transition to toddler bed arrangements, and their cribs no longer prevent them from leaving their rooms and seeking parents, guess who will be joining you in the middle of the night? Although we completely understand parents' discomfort with the idea of just not showing up to their crying infant in the night (known as *extinguishing*), this is exactly the approach I (Masha) ultimately had to take with my daughter. I had just returned back to a full teaching load after having my daughter (then slightly over 1 year old) teaching our graduate child/adolescent disorder treatment course. I quickly learned that my daughter's pattern of waking up two to three times a night multiple times a week could in fact be diagnosed as a sleep disorder. I also realized that a highly reliable treatment involved withdrawing all reinforcement during the night, stopping to come to her "cold turkey" in an effort to extinguish this now highly disruptive behavior pattern. I talked to my husband about this insight and our options, and we decided we would start the extinguishing protocol over the upcoming spring break, hoping to get the worst nights out of the way while I wasn't teaching. Well, it took 3 weeks, just like the studies indicated.

Needless to say, there were some terrible nights once I returned to the regular teaching schedule, and many times we wished for a sound-proof room for our child. Also, I did feel like a terrible mother a lot. I tried to stay grounded in the goal of sleep independence, which my husband and I both embraced, reminding myself that my child was safe. This was not easy by any stretch of the imagination, but it worked, and 3 exhausting weeks later my daughter began sleeping through the night. One point worth adding is that some parents are hesitant to extinguish waking/crying behavior because they are concerned this approach will ruin their relationship with the child or diminish the child's attachment security. There is no scientific evidence that this happens, and it did not happen with me and my daughter. My sense is that as long as you are sensitive and responsive to the child in other aspects of your interactions, setting sleep-related limits does not lead to adverse effects.

I (Liliana) took a different approach. My husband and I felt better with successive approximations (described in Chapter 8, on working with inflexible children). First, we decided to stop feeding our children during the night (when they were old enough). We did that for about 10 to 14 days. Then, we limited the comfort we provided by not picking up our crying babies but rather just putting a hand on or near them to calm them down. After about a couple weeks of that, we went into their room and provided verbal assurances but didn't provide physical contact. Last, we would stand in the doorway and provide verbal assurances before we finally stopped responding. Also, there were a few things that contributed to challenges with this approach. Our oldest daughter used a pacifier, and she would often wake and become distressed at night because she couldn't find one of the four pacifiers we put in her bed. She didn't sleep well until we weaned her off of a pacifier altogether. Our youngest daughter's crib was in our room because we did not have a separate room for her. She often soothed herself by pulling herself up in her crib and looking at us, sometimes calling out for us. But by the last steps, we were able to ignore those bids for our attention. This approach of successive approximations takes longer than the approach Masha used, and it can be very tiring. It worked for us because my husband and I took turns, each of us getting some sleep at least every other night, which worked out OK with our work schedules.

We (Liliana and Masha) have described the two approaches we used in detail to illustrate that there is no one right way to support babies sleeping through the night and, whatever you choose to do, it helps to understand the principles of behavior reinforcement. It may also be worth mentioning that most babies around the world do not sleep independently, that this is a relatively recent development in family routines that is mainstream only in certain cultures and has been linked with individualistic, autonomy-related values. If you desire separate sleeping arrangements, embracing this as a socialization goal (i.e., something you want to accomplish as a parent), and can achieve such independence by the start of the second year of life, you are probably in a pretty good place when the toddler bed makes its appearance. Even so, there may be disruptions in a regular sleep pattern because of travel or unanticipated events. Getting back to a good sleep habit is important and should be described as such to now-verbal toddlers and preschoolers.

In general, a regular calming bedtime routine will go a long way toward promoting a good sleep habit across the life span. This means developing steps leading to sleep that are conducive to relaxation, and for young children this often starts with a bath. Even with no bath, changing into pajamas or another comfy outfit can help. Some kind of a relaxing activity, like singing calm songs, reading, or telling stories, also is useful. Screen time is not relaxing and actually disrupts sleep. Consistency is important with sleep as well—doing the same or similar things every night at about the same time is critical.

Also, research indicates that children who fall asleep outside of their bed tend to struggle with sleep problems, so letting your child settle into a chair or a couch before transitioning to bed is likely not a good solution in the long run. The advice is surprisingly similar for adolescents who are challenged by developmental shifts in their sleep patterns. Having a consistent pattern of bed and rise time is key. Although it is not possible to dictate a sleep time, having an established bedtime creates the foundation for a regular sleep time. The same goes for wake times, and having wildly different wake time expectations (e.g., a 6:30 a.m. wake time on weekdays and a noon wake time on weekends) is definitely dysregulating. Of course, adolescents require greater autonomy, but it may be possible to get them to engage in maintaining consistency by providing information about the importance of a regular schedule, emphasizing its benefits in terms of mood and quality of interactions, as well as educational activities.

MEALTIME ROUTINE

Spoiler alert—when it comes to avoiding mealtime struggles, routines and consistency are going to be important as well. Get in the habit of having a family mealtime on a regular basis, keeping it as stress free as possible. Maybe planning meals everyone is going to enjoy is the right approach, and this doesn't mean just Mom trying to please everyone with her cuisine creations. Regardless of how meals are prepared and the labor around mealtime shared, having a meal together as a family is highly recommended. In fact, it is just as important to adolescents as younger children who are still learning about eating and gaining independence in this activity. It turns out that having family meals is one way to ensure that adolescents, who tend to make poor food choices with their friends, have adequate nutrition. Despite its importance, family mealtime is also known for creating conflict, such as when parents disagree about how to handle their picky eater's refusal to eat, or fighting among siblings at the dinner table. When this pattern emerges it is critical for parents/caregivers to get on the same page about their mealtime goals, providing structure without resorting to yelling and coercion. Having a child skip a meal could ultimately be acceptable, as long as there are other opportunities for getting appropriate nutrition and there is a rationale for why access to food was limited during this particular meal. In other words, it should not be a mystery to a child why all of the dishes are being taken away and they've missed out on dinner or some other meal. Connect the dots—"You need to eat when everyone else in the family is eating. We'll try again at breakfast." Don't be afraid to use a timer to help your child understand how long they have to work on their plate, for example. With children who have difficulty with new foods, it's a good idea to baby-step into new textures and tastes. For example, you can have a rule that a child has to try something, but they don't need to finish it if they don't like it. A caveat is warranted about the fact that many children who are diagnosed with an autism spectrum disorder are picky eaters and struggle with textures. In this situation, it's always best to get additional guidance from your pediatrician or family doctor, or a child mental health professional.

Because this book is about temperament, it is important to point out that, for children who are easily frustrated, reactive to novelty, or struggle with regulation, sleep and mealtime routines may be more challenging. For example, children who are more distress prone are more likely to awaken and require parental intervention to get back to sleep (recall that everyone wakes up in the night, and "good sleepers" can get themselves back to sleep). Those who hesitate in the face of novelty may be especially challenged by an introduction of new foods or new mealtime routines, such as eating at a restaurant with others present. As you become more mindful of your child's temperament, and we hope this book will help you do that, you will be able to anticipate the aspects of daily routine and activities that are going to be most challenging for them, coming up with a plan ahead of time, and then staying grounded in your goals and providing nurturance in the face of distress if needed.

GETTING OUT THE DOOR ON TIME

Getting out the door on time, especially in the morning, can be a challenge for children with different temperament profiles, for different reasons. The inflexible child may struggle the most if some aspect of the morning routine is disrupted or they have to make choices for which they are not prepared. As with prior daily routine situations, the primary advice concerning getting out the door is to have a routine, preferably getting as much out of the way (e.g., outfit choices, making lunches) the night before as possible. If something does need to change, this deviation should be discussed ahead of time as well, if at all possible. Of course, sometimes surprises happen, and we have to make adjustments on the fly. If one of these morning surprises pops up, it may be a good time to lower your expectations. It's OK to bring a lunch that may not be ideal in terms of nutrition, wear an outfit that is not as consistent with weather conditions as one would like, and so on. Having worked with parents of preschool-age children who struggled with this situation, I (Masha) can tell you that it is just fine for a child to go to preschool or day care in pajamas on occasion. After all, they will typically have clothes to change into at their day care or preschool, and taking a shortcut on getting dressed can make a difference between being on time for drop-off—and, subsequently, work—or not.

It is also helpful to build in a reinforcement for getting out the door on time. This is particularly true for reward-oriented children, that is, those who tend to be easily frustrated or impulsive. For example, let your child lock the house door or unlock the car (some kids love keys and buttons!), but only if everyone is ready and at the door at the specified time. Or allow your child to select the music during the car ride to school if they were ready on time. Little rewards like these can get everyone off to a more pleasant start in the morning. Collaborate with your child in coming up with the rewards, and they will work even more effectively.

HOMEWORK

Yes, it's also good to have a homework routine and to be consistent. If getting your child to complete homework is a struggle, it may be useful to reconsider the order of activities. You might remember that, as we noted earlier, it's always easier to switch from a less desirable activity to a more desirable activity, or at least to transition from one activity to the next that are not vastly different. If your reward-oriented or fearless child gets home from school and immediately has access to screen time (for example), it will likely be a challenge to get them to switch to reading or math problems. With a child who presents with this type of a temperament profile it would be more effective to have screen time serve as a reinforcer, following homework activities. We are not suggesting that kids should not get a break after school! It is definitely a good idea to do something different after getting home, maybe something active after sitting so much during the day. However, most desirable activities, such as video games and YouTube scrolling, or playing outside with the neighborhood kids, are better saved for after the homework is out of the way. This is a good time to note that if your child is really struggling with schoolwork, and that these difficulties are not remedied by these suggested approaches or by additional support during homework, it would likely be helpful to have a formal evaluation addressing learning difficulties, which are sometimes a result of diagnosable learning disorders in reading, writing, and math.

For children who have trouble persisting with their homework, it might be helpful to build in break times every 15 or 20 minutes. A break can be 5 minutes of an enjoyable, refreshing activity (listening to music, playing an instrument, dancing, tossing a ball to your dog, getting fresh air, having a snack outside, etc.). This should not be a highly desirable activity that is hard to disengage from (e.g., video games or other time on devices). Instead, this should provide a short "brain break" that can help your child return to their work for another 15 or 20 minutes. It helps to set a timer to further structure your child's time. And, over time, as your child builds their ability to focus attention and persist, the amount of work time can be increased a little at a time, for example, from 15 minutes to 20 minutes, and then later to 25 minutes.

CHORES/CLEANING THEIR ROOM

I (Masha) was recently talking to a friend who said she finally got her son to clean his room, and they discovered unopened gifts from the previous holiday season, and the clothes didn't fit him anymore. She was not pleased. Although it's probably not possible to avoid all chore and cleaning disappointments with teenagers, it is a good idea to get a regular routine for household chores and room cleaning established early. If chores are routine daily or weekly events, it is far more likely that these will get done. Failure to complete certain chores may have natural consequences, which might be sufficient for some children to do what is expected. But these natural consequences might not work for other children. For example, having a messy room might be embarrassing if a friend stops by, and not having a clean outfit for school because the laundry was not done can be frustrating and inconvenient. However, if your child is not embarrassed by a messy room, or happy to go to school in stinky clothes—and some are—these natural consequences will not have the desired effect. In these cases, building in reinforcements for completing chores might be necessary.

Children who are easily frustrated or impulsive are often reluctant to do chores because they take longer than they want or require a greater attention to detail than what they had anticipated. In my (Liliana's) family, we schedule household chores to be completed on Saturdays, with each person signing up for their tasks and being required to have all chores done by a specified afternoon time (giving them autonomy in deciding when they complete the chores), and we have done this since my children were very young. Despite this, my reward-oriented son consistently complained about having to do chores even while he was doing them. Having a routine helps reduce challenges with compliance. Greater persistence with chores can be achieved with clear expectations, consistency, and reinforcement. When a child is able to complete chores as instructed, something desirable happens. It doesn't have to be screen time, but it could be. Our favorite reinforcers are social ones, like playing a board game your child enjoys, or taking a dog on a special outing. This is something I (Masha) do because our Shih Tzu enjoys going out to local stores that are dog friendly, and it's a lot of fun for my daughter.

It is also important to be very clear about what is expected for each chore. If you direct your child to clean their room, and they say they are done, but you still see a mess, it might be that you have different expectations about what a clean room is. However, if you provide scaffolding around the chore—that is, break down the task to its specific parts—it's easier for both the parent and the child to understand what needs to be done. Rather than "Clean your room," you can make a checklist of what it means to clean a room (e.g., put dirty clothes in the laundry, pick up all toys and put them in the toy bin, put all trash in the trash can, make your bed, dust your shelves, sweep/vacuum the floor). This makes it clear to the child what is expected, and it gives both the parent and child a structure around deciding when the task is done. A checklist like this can be used for other household chores, regularly required tasks like homework, and other situations as well. The more clear and specific the instructions are, the easier it will be for your child to be successful.

CONCLUSION

One message we hope you got as you have read this book is that different strategies work differently with children depending on their temperament. Although we have emphasized similar domains of parenting throughout (presence, warmth, balance, and consistency), their applications vary depending on the individual child's temperament profile. Moreover, these approaches can be adapted depending on cultural and family values and considerations, and parents should not feel stuck with strategies that do not seem to be consistent with theirs, or are not feasible for them.

AFTERWORD

BUILDING SOCIAL AND EMOTIONAL COMPETENCE, JOY, AND WELL-BEING

In writing this book, our goal was to share insights based on the extensive body of research on children's temperament and parenting, together with our clinical and personal experiences. Our hope is that parents and other adults caring for and working with children will gain a better understanding of the unique temperament qualities of the children in their lives and how to support positive social, emotional, and behavioral development for those children. With these tools, we believe parents can be more effective in supporting their children's social–emotional development, promoting their well-being, and enjoying their relationships with their children more fully.

Parents often convey their confusion and frustration with the fact that typical parenting advice doesn't always work with their children, and this is not surprising because parenting is not "one size fits all." We have experienced this firsthand with our own children, and in this book we wanted to convey how core parenting principles—that is, being present, warm, balanced, and consistent—can be implemented differently to provide a better fit for children with challenging temperament profiles. Gaining an understanding of individual differences and unique profiles in children's emotional reactivity and regulation can help parents understand their children more fully, personalize their responses to their children's emotions and behaviors, and troubleshoot the strategies that are not working as well as hoped.

Research tells us that children with certain temperament characteristics, like being highly fearful, easily frustrated, impulsive, or inflexible, or any combination of these, are more likely to develop social, emotional, or behavioral problems. This happens primarily not because of their biological risk for this but because of how they process and react to their experiences—in particular, stressful experiences. It happens because children with these characteristics in particular respond differently to the people, parents, teachers, peers, and others they interact with, and people respond differently to them in turn. Also, because of these evocative properties of temperament, some children find themselves in risky or dangerous situations, or they miss out on typical or enriching developmental experiences.

Conversely, these very same characteristics also have positive outcomes. Fearful children are more careful and responsive to guidance and more interested in words of wisdom you have to share about staying safe and making good choices. Easily frustrated and impulsive children can more easily relish rewarding experiences and are often eager to participate. Fearless children partake in more exhilarating activities, which could be really fun for families that enjoy skiing, mountain biking, amusement parks, and so on. What is particularly encouraging about this is that children with temperament characteristics that increase their risk for developing problems can be supported in ways that bring out the best of their qualities and in ways that build their social and emotional competence as well as their joy and well-being. Our main goal in writing this book was to describe what this support looks like and ways in which it can be offered to children with different temperament profiles, based on relevant scientific research.

We also hope that a deeper understanding of our children's temperament styles and some of the recommended parenting strategies will enhance parents' joy in parenting and enjoyment of their children. Most important, we hope that parents feel validated in their experiences with their children, both the challenges and the joys. This book is an invitation to parents and other adults who care for children to tap into their own wisdom and trust themselves in figuring out the strategies that will work best for the children in their lives. We hope that by parenting with your child's temperament in mind you will feel more confident and competent in navigating challenges and have more opportunities to enjoy and celebrate your child's strengths.

APPENDIX A

CHILD TEMPERAMENT ASSESSMENT

In this appendix, we offer some guidance geared toward understanding your child's temperament characteristics. We provide some statements that describe each temperament characteristic, and you will decide how well those statements describe your child. You will then be able to score your child on each dimension and record their scores on the scales to get an idea of which characteristics are higher and lower for your child. There are no cutoffs for "high" or "low" for these dimensions because children can be anywhere along the continuum and still be within the "normal range." Everyone has a temperament and lands somewhere on each of the dimensions—this is not diagnostic of a condition or a disorder.

SCORING THE TEMPERAMENT–REACTIVITY AND REGULATION REFLECTION

You are going to compute an average for each of the temperament dimensions we described in Chapter 2. Once you have your child's scores computed, you can look back to that chapter for information on low and high scores. First, write the value you gave to each item in the last column, add up those scores in the last column, and divide that total by the number of items. For the Effortful Control score, average your Attention Focusing and Inhibitory Control scores (add them up and divide by 2).

TEMPERAMENT–REACTIVITY AND REGULATION REFLECTION

These statements describe children's reactions to a number of situations. Consider your child's age as you respond to these items. Some of the items might not directly apply to your child's developmental stage, but reply with your best estimate for their age. We would like you to tell us what your child's reaction is likely to be in those situations. There are no "correct" ways of reacting; children differ in their reactions. Please read each statement and decide how true the description is of your child's reaction *within the past 6 months.*

Attention focusing	Never true	Rarely true	Slightly true	Pretty true	Often true	Always true	Score
1. Concentrates strongly when reading or looking at a book, drawing, or coloring in a book.	0	1	2	3	4	5	
2. When building or putting something together, becomes very involved in what they are doing and works for a long time.	0	1	2	3	4	5	
3. Is easily distracted when listening to a story.	5	4	3	2	1	0	
4. Has difficulty tuning out background noise and concentrating when trying to read or study.	5	4	3	2	1	0	
Average: Add up the scores and divide by 4.							

Fearfulness	Never true	Rarely true	Slightly true	Pretty true	Often true	Always true	
1. Is afraid of the dark or loud noises.	0	1	2	3	4	5	
2. Is afraid to do things or go places for the first time.	0	1	2	3	4	5	
3. Is frightened by "monsters" or scary scenes in shows or movies.	0	1	2	3	4	5	
4. Is often worried about getting into trouble.	0	1	2	3	4	5	
5. Is afraid of being late to activities and appointments.	0	1	2	3	4	5	
Average: Add up the scores and divide by 5.							

Frustration	Never true	Rarely true	Slightly true	Pretty true	Often true	Always true	Score
1. Gets quite frustrated when prevented from doing something they want to do or getting something they want.	0	1	2	3	4	5	
2. Gets angry when they can't find something they want to play with.	0	1	2	3	4	5	
3. Gets angry when called in from play before they are ready to stop.	0	1	2	3	4	5	
4. Gets irritated when they have to stop doing something enjoyable.	0	1	2	3	4	5	
Average: Add up the scores and divide by 4.							

High-intensity pleasure	Never true	Rarely true	Slightly true	Pretty true	Often true	Always true	Score
1. Likes going down high slides or other adventurous activities.	0	1	2	3	4	5	
2. Enjoys activities like being chased, spun around, etc.	0	1	2	3	4	5	
3. Would like to ski or bike fast down a steep hill.	0	1	2	3	4	5	
Average: Add up the scores and divide by 3.							

Impulsivity	Never true	Rarely true	Slightly true	Pretty true	Often true	Always true	Score
1. Often rushes into new situations.	0	1	2	3	4	5	
2. Usually rushes into an activity without thinking about it.	0	1	2	3	4	5	
3. Says the first thing that comes to mind, without stopping to think about it.	0	1	2	3	4	5	
4. Is not very careful and cautious in crossing streets or parking lots or similar situations.	0	1	2	3	4	5	
5. When seeing a toy or game they want, is eager to have it right then.	0	1	2	3	4	5	
Average: Add up the scores and divide by 5.							

Inflexibility	Never true	Rarely true	Slightly true	Pretty true	Often true	Always true	
1. Needs things to remain the same.	0	1	2	3	4	5	
2. Dislikes when things are unpredictable.	0	1	2	3	4	5	
3. Resists having to change the way they do things.	0	1	2	3	4	5	
4. Reluctant to try new things.	0	1	2	3	4	5	
Average: Add up the scores and divide by 4.							

Inhibitory control	Never true	Rarely true	Slightly true	Pretty true	Often true	Always true	
1. Is good at following instructions.	0	1	2	3	4	5	
2. Approaches places they have been told are dangerous slowly and cautiously.	0	1	2	3	4	5	
3. Can wait before entering into new activities if they are asked to.	0	1	2	3	4	5	
4. Can easily stop an activity when they are told "no."	0	1	2	3	4	5	
5. Usually stops and thinks things over before deciding to do something.	0	1	2	3	4	5	
Average: Add up the scores and divide by 5.							

Positive affect	Never true	Rarely true	Slightly true	Pretty true	Often true	Always true	Score
1. Sometimes smiles or giggles when playing by themselves.	0	1	2	3	4	5	
2. Often laughs out loud in play with other children.	0	1	2	3	4	5	
3. Smiles and laughs while playing or working on projects.	0	1	2	3	4	5	
4. Is generally cheerful.	0	1	2	3	4	5	
Average: Add up the scores and divide by 4.							

Reward approach/anticipation	Never true	Rarely true	Slightly true	Pretty true	Often true	Always true	Score
1. Gets so worked up before an exciting event that they have trouble sitting still.	0	1	2	3	4	5	
2. Becomes very excited before an outing (e.g., park, party).	0	1	2	3	4	5	
3. Has trouble waiting calmly for upcoming desserts like ice cream or cookies.	0	1	2	3	4	5	
Average: Add up the scores and divide by 3.							

Soothability–emotion regulation	Never true	Rarely true	Slightly true	Pretty true	Often true	Always true	Score
1. When angry about something, tends to stay upset for ten minutes or longer.	5	4	3	2	1	0	
2. Is very difficult to soothe when they have become upset.	5	4	3	2	1	0	
3. When they become upset, they can return to what they were doing or need to be doing fairly quickly.	0	1	2	3	4	5	
Average: Add up the scores and divide by 3.							

Note. This screening tool has been adapted from research measures but should not be used for research purposes. The original published measures should be used for research. This assessment is based on items from multiple instruments:

- The Children's Behavior Questionnaire is from "Investigations of Temperament at Three to Seven Years: The Children's Behavior Questionnaire," by M. K. Rothbart, S. A. Ahadi, K. L. Hershey, and P. Fisher, 2001, *Child Development*, 72(5), pp. 1394–1408 (https://doi.org/10.1111/1467-8624.00355). Copyright 2001 by M. K. Rothbart. Items reprinted with permission.
- *The Early Adolescent Temperament Questionnaire—Revised, Short Form*, by L. K. Ellis and M. K. Rothbart, April 2001. Poster presented at the Biennial Meeting of the Society for Research in Child Development, Minneapolis, MN, USA (http://education-webfiles.s3-website-us-west-2.amazonaws.com/childcare/pdf/instrumental_docs/Early%20Adolescent%20Temperament%20Q-Revised%20Adolescent%20Short%20Form%20ID.pdf). Copyright 2001 by M. Rothbart. Items reprinted with permission.
- The Behavioral Inflexibility Scale is from "Development of the Behavioral Inflexibility Scale for Children With Autism Spectrum Disorder and Other Developmental Disabilities," by L. Lecavalier, J. Bodfish, C. Harrop, A. Whitten, D. Jones, J. Pritchett, R. Faldowski, and B. Boyd, 2020, *Autism Research, 13*(3), pp. 489–499 (https://doi.org/10.1002/aur.2257). CC BY 4.0 DEED.

Notes to Consider:

Effortful Control: Average your Attention Focusing and Inhibitory Control Scores (add them up and divide by 2). Children can show better effortful control capacity when they have good attention regulation or good inhibitory control, or both.

Reward Approach/Anticipation: If your child scores high(er) on impulsivity or frustration, consider their Reward Approach/Anticipation score, which might help you understand the roots of their impulsivity and frustration. If the Reward Approach/Anticipation score is lower, then impulsivity might be more related to their tendency toward high-intensity pleasure and/or low fear.

Soothability: Your child's ability to be soothed or to soothe themselves might reflect their respiratory sinus arrhythmia (discussed in Chapter 4) or better effortful control.

Temperament Profile

Temperament	0	1	2	3	4	5
Fearfulness						
Frustration						
Impulsivity						
Reward Approach						
High-intensity Pleasure						
Positive Affect						
Effortful Control						
Attention Focusing						
Inhibitory Control						
Soothability						
Inflexibility						

Check the box with the score for each dimension.

APPENDIX B

PARENTING SELF-REFLECTION

In this appendix you have an opportunity to reflect on your parenting behaviors. We have included statements that give you an idea of what behaviors are associated with each of the four core parenting principles we described in Chapters 9 through 12. You can respond to the items and score yourself on each behavior to help you get a profile of your parenting.

SCORING THE PARENTING SELF-REFLECTION

You are going to compute an average for each parenting dimension. First, write the value you gave to each item in the last column, add up those scores in the last column, and divide by the number of items.

PARENTING SELF-REFLECTION

Please describe yourself as a parent. Consider your child's age as you respond to these items. Some of the items might not directly apply to your child's developmental stage, but reply with your best estimate for their age. Decide how much the statements below describe how you generally have been *during the past 6 months*. Respond whether the statement is "never like you," "always like you," or somewhere in between.

Be Present

This refers to paying attention, listening, noticing, and engaging with your child calmly responding without overreacting.

Mindfulness in parenting	Never true	Rarely true	Slightly true	Pretty true	Often true	Always true	Score
1. You find yourself not being as attentive as you could be with your child, because your mind is preoccupied with other things.	5	4	3	2	1	0	
2. When you're upset with your child, you notice how you are feeling before you take action.	0	1	2	3	4	5	
3. You notice how changes in your child's mood affect your mood.	0	1	2	3	4	5	
4. You often react too quickly to what your child says or does.	5	4	3	2	1	0	

5. You are aware of how your moods affect the way you treat your child.	0	1	2	3	4	5	
6. Even though it sometimes makes you uncomfortable, you allow your child to express themselves.	0	1	2	3	4	5	
7. You rush through activities with your child without being fully attentive to them.	5	4	3	2	1	0	
8. When you become upset with your child, you are able to calm down and not have it affect your mood or the way in which you care for your child.	0	1	2	3	4	5	
Average: Add up your score and divide by 8.							

Be Warm

This refers to the quality of your relationship with your child and includes affection, acceptance, and low levels of rejection and hostility.

Acceptance	Never true	Rarely true	Slightly true	Pretty true	Often true	Always true	Score
1. You are not interested in changing your child, but like them the way they are.	0	1	2	3	4	5	
2. You see your child's good points more than their faults.	0	1	2	3	4	5	
3. You smile at your child very often.	0	1	2	3	4	5	
4. You make your child feel better when they are upset or worried.	0	1	2	3	4	5	
5. You enjoy doing things with your child.	0	1	2	3	4	5	
6. You cheer your child up when they are sad.	0	1	2	3	4	5	
7. You often speak to your child about the good things they do.	0	1	2	3	4	5	
8. You are proud of the things your child does.	0	1	2	3	4	5	
Average: Add up the scores and divide by 8.							

Rejection/Hostility	Never true	Rarely true	Slightly true	Pretty true	Often true	Always true	Score
1. You are not very patient with your child.	0	1	2	3	4	5	
2. You think your child's ideas are silly.	0	1	2	3	4	5	
3. You say your child is a big problem.	0	1	2	3	4	5	
4. You are always reprimanding or nagging your child.	0	1	2	3	4	5	
5. You complain to your child about what they do.	0	1	2	3	4	5	
6. You get angry about little things your child does.	0	1	2	3	4	5	
7. You often blow up when your child bothers you.	0	1	2	3	4	5	
8. You act as though your child is in the way.	0	1	2	3	4	5	
Average: Add up the scores and divide by 8.							

Be Balanced

This is a combination of stepping in to respond to your child's emotions or needs while also stepping back and allowing your child autonomy when appropriate.

Responsiveness	Never true	Rarely true	Slightly true	Pretty true	Often true	Always true	Score
1. You pay attention to what your child is noticing or is interested in.	0	1	2	3	4	5	
2. You respond to your child when they are upset or crying.	0	1	2	3	4	5	
3. You console your child when they are upset by holding or hugging them, touching or getting physically close/offering physical comfort.	0	1	2	3	4	5	
4. You listen to your child or sit with them when they are upset.	0	1	2	3	4	5	

5. You hug or hold your child, or sit close to them, when it looks like they want you to.	0	1	2	3	4	5	
6. If there is something that scares or frustrates your child, you try to figure out how to help.	0	1	2	3	4	5	
7. When there is something your child enjoys doing, you try to do it with them as often as possible.	0	1	2	3	4	5	
8. If something is making your child uncomfortable, you try to help them.	0	1	2	3	4	5	
Average: Add up your scores and divide by 8.							

Autonomy support with guidance	Never true	Rarely true	Slightly true	Pretty true	Often true	Always true	Score
1. You let your child decide how to do things.	0	1	2	3	4	5	
2. You support your child in trying out their ideas.	0	1	2	3	4	5	
3. You ask your child how the two of you should do things or work together to solve problems.	0	1	2	3	4	5	
4. You try to understand how your child sees things.	0	1	2	3	4	5	
5. You offer ideas or tips for how to solve a problem.	0	1	2	3	4	5	
6. You offer your child choices and give your child a choice of what to do when possible.	0	1	2	3	4	5	
Average: Add up your score and divide by 6.							

Be Consistent

This refers to having clear, developmentally appropriate expectations, limits, and rules that you implement consistently.

Consistent limit-setting	Never true	Rarely true	Slightly true	Pretty true	Often true	Always true	Score
1. You soon forgot a rule you have made.	5	4	3	2	1	0	
2. You punish your child for doing something one day but you ignore it the next day.	5	4	3	2	1	0	
3. You sometimes allow your child to do things you say are wrong.	5	4	3	2	1	0	
4. It depends upon your mood whether a rule is enforced or not.	5	4	3	2	1	0	
5. You only keep rules when it suits you.	5	4	3	2	1	0	
6. You don't get your child things unless they ask for them over and over again.	5	4	3	2	1	0	

(*continues*)

Consistent limit-setting	Never true	Rarely true	Slightly true	Pretty true	Often true	Always true	Score
7. You insist that your child follow a rule one day and then you forget about it the next.	5	4	3	2	1	0	
8. You frequently change the rules your child is supposed to follow.	5	4	3	2	1	0	
Average: Add up the scores and divide by 8.							

Note. This screening tool has been adapted from research measures but should not be used for research purposes. The original published measures should be used for research. This assessment is based on items from multiple inventories:

- The Child's Report of Parenting Parental Behavior Inventory–Parent Version: (Teleki, Powell, & Dodder, 1982). "Factor Analysis of Reports of Parental Behavior by Children Living in Divorced and Married Families," by J. K. Teleki, J. A. Powell, and R. A. Dodder, 1982, *The Journal of Psychology*, *112*(2), 295–302 (https://doi.org/10.1080/00223980.1982.9915387). Copyright 1982 by Taylor & Francis. Items reprinted with permission.
- The Parental Responsiveness Scale for Infants: From Anikiej-Wiczenbach, P., & Kaźmierczak, M. (2021). "Validation of the Parental Responsiveness Scale," by P. Anikiej-Wiczenbach and M. Kaźmierczak, 2021, *Current Issues in Personality Psychology*, *9*(3), 258–266, Copyright © Institute of Psychology, University of Gdansk. Items reprinted via the Creative Commons Attribution-NonCommercial-ShareAlike 4.0 International (CC BY-NC-SA 4.0) License (http://creativecommons.org/licenses/by-nc-sa/4.0/).
- The Mindful Parenting in Infancy Scale: From Gartstein, M. A. (2021). "Development and Validation of the Mindful Parenting in Infancy Scale (MPIS)," by M. A. Gartstein, 2021, *Infancy*, *26*(5), 705–723 (https://doi.org/10.1111/infa.12417). Copyright 2021 by Wiley-Blackwell. Items reprinted with permission.

Parenting Profile

Parenting	0	1	2	3	4	5
Presence						
Warmth						
Acceptance						
Rejection						
Balance						
Responsive						
Autonomy						
Consistent						

Check the box with your score on each of the dimensions.

SUPPORTIVE RESEARCH

These works informed the content of this book.

Arcus, D. (2001). Inhibited and uninhibited children: Biology in the social context. In T. D. Wachs & G. A. Kohnstamm (Eds.), *Temperament in context* (pp. 43–60). Erlbaum.

Beauchaine, T. P. (2015). Respiratory sinus arrhythmia: A transdiagnostic biomarker of emotion dysregulation and psychopathology. *Current Opinion in Psychology*, *3*, 43–47. https://doi.org/10.1016/j.copsyc.2015.01.017

Caspi, A., Harrington, H., Milne, B., Amell, J. W., Theodore, R. F., & Moffitt, T. E. (2003). Children's behavioral styles at age 3 are linked to their adult personality traits at age 26. *Journal of Personality*, *71*(4), 495–514. https://doi.org/10.1111/1467-6494.7104001

Chamberlain, S. R., Leppink, E. W., Redden, S. A., & Grant, J. E. (2016). Are obsessive–compulsive symptoms impulsive, compulsive or both? *Comprehensive Psychiatry*, *68*, 111–118. https://doi.org/10.1016/j.comppsych.2016.04.010

Conway, A. (2020). Longitudinal associations between parenting and inattention, impulsivity, and delay of gratification in preschool-aged children: The role of temperamental difficultness and toddler attention focusing. *Developmental Neuropsychology*, *45*(5), 309–329. https://doi.org/10.1080/87565641.2020.1797042

Degnan, K. A., Hane, A. A., Henderson, H. A., Moas, O. L., Reeb-Sutherland, B. C., & Fox, N. A. (2011). Longitudinal stability of temperamental

exuberance and social–emotional outcomes in early childhood. *Developmental Psychology*, *47*(3), 765–780. https://doi.org/10.1037/a0021316
Dougherty, L. R., Klein, D. N., Olino, T. M., Dyson, M., & Rose, S. (2009). Increased waking salivary cortisol and depression risk in preschoolers: The role of maternal history of melancholic depression and early child temperament. *The Journal of Child Psychology and Psychiatry*, *50*(12), 1495–1503. https://doi.org/10.1111/j.1469-7610.2009.02116.x
Eisenberg, N., Taylor, Z. E., Widaman, K. F., & Spinrad, T. L. (2015). Externalizing symptoms, effortful control, and intrusive parenting: A test of bidirectional longitudinal relations during early childhood. *Development and Psychopathology*, *27*(4, Pt. 1), 953–968. https://doi.org/10.1017/S0954579415000620
Gartstein, M. A., Putnam, S. P., Aaron, E., & Rothbart, M. K. (2016). Temperament and personality. In S. Matzman (Ed.), *Oxford handbook of treatment processes and outcomes in counseling psychology* (pp. 11–41). Oxford University Press.
Gilliom, M., & Shaw, D. S. (2004). Codevelopment of externalizing and internalizing problems in early childhood. *Development and Psychopathology*, *16*(2), 313–333. https://doi.org/10.1017/S0954579404044530
Gunnar, M. R., Sebanc, A. M., Tout, K., Donzella, B., & van Dulmen, M. M. H. (2003). Peer rejection, temperament, and cortisol activity in preschoolers. *Developmental Psychobiology*, *43*(4), 346–368.
Klein, M. R., Lengua, L. J., Thompson, S. F., Moran, L., Ruberry, E. J., Kiff, C., & Zalewski, M. (2018). Bidirectional relations between temperament and parenting predicting preschool-age children's adjustment. *Journal of Clinical Child & Adolescent Psychology*, *47*(Supp. 1), S113–S126. https://doi.org/10.1080/15374416.2016.1169537
McQuillan, M. E., & Bates, J. E. (2017). Parental stress and child temperament. In K. Deater-Deckard & R. Panneton (Eds.), *Parental stress and early child development: Adaptive and maladaptive outcomes* (pp. 75–106). Springer International. https://doi.org/10.1007/978-3-319-55376-4_4
Mobley, C. E., & Pullis, M. E. (1991). Temperament and behavioral adjustment in preschool children. *Early Childhood Research Quarterly*, *6*(4), 577–586. https://doi.org/10.1016/0885-2006(91)90038-M
Olson, S. L., Bates, J. E., & Bayles, K. (1990). Early antecedents of childhood impulsivity: The role of parent–child interaction, cognitive competence, and temperament. *Journal of Abnormal Child Psychology*, *18*(3), 317–334. https://doi.org/10.1007/BF00916568

Paterson, G., & Sanson, A. (1999). The association of behavioural adjustment to temperament, parenting and family characteristics among 5-year-old children. *Social Development*, *8*(3), 293–309. https://doi.org/10.1111/1467-9507.00097

Peng, B., Hu, N., Yu, H., Xiao, H., & Luo, J. (2021). Parenting style and adolescent mental health: The chain mediating effects of self-esteem and psychological inflexibility. *Frontiers in Psychology*, *12*, 738170. https://doi.org/10.3389/fpsyg.2021.738170

Rabinowitz, J. A., Drabick, D. A., Reynolds, M. D., Clark, D. B., & Olino, T. M. (2016). Child temperamental flexibility moderates the relation between positive parenting and adolescent adjustment. *Journal of Applied Developmental Psychology*, *43*, 43–53. https://doi.org/10.1016/j.appdev.2015.12.006

Reznik, S. J., & Allen, J. J. B. (2018). Frontal asymmetry as a mediator and moderator of emotion: An updated review. *Psychophysiology*, *55*(1), e12965. https://doi.org/10.1111/psyp.12965

Rothbart, M. K. (2011). *Becoming who we are: Temperament and personality in development*. Guilford Press.

Sanson, A., & Rothbart, M. K. (1995). Child temperament and parenting. In M. H. Bornstein (Ed.), *Handbook of parenting, Vol. 4: Applied and practical parenting* (pp. 299–321). Erlbaum.

Spinrad, T. L., & Gal, D. E. (2018). Fostering prosocial behavior and empathy in young children. *Current Opinion in Psychology*, *20*, 40–44. https://doi.org/10.1016/j.copsyc.2017.08.004

Wang, F. L., Eisenberg, N., Valiente, C., & Spinrad, T. L. (2016). Role of temperament in early adolescent pure and co-occurring internalizing and externalizing problems using a bifactor model: Moderation by parenting and gender. *Development and Psychopathology*, *28*(4, Pt. 2), 1487–1504. https://doi.org/10.1017/S0954579415001224

Williams, K. E., Ciarrochi, J., & Heaven, P. C. (2012). Inflexible parents, inflexible kids: A 6-year longitudinal study of parenting style and the development of psychological flexibility in adolescents. *Journal of Youth and Adolescence*, *41*(8), 1053–1066. https://doi.org/10.1007/s10964-012-9744-0

REFERENCES

Anikiej-Wiczenbach, P., & Kazmierczak, M. (2021). Validation of the Parental Responsiveness Scale. *Current Issues in Personality Psychology*, *9*(3), 258–266. https://doi.org/10.5114/cipp.2021.104800

Blue, A. (2019, November 15). *We learn best when we fail 15% of the time, according to a study*. World Economic Forum. https://www.weforum.org/agenda/2019/11/learn-best-fail-85-time?fbclid=IwAR1NlTectw14F_qguKPeYE-fclVD0E8TYzMeaezPkysCYLMCqdUjfV1gCMA

Buss, K. A., & Kiel, E. J. (2011). Do maternal protective behaviors alleviate toddlers' fearful distress? *International Journal of Behavioral Development*, *35*(2), 136–143. https://doi.org/10.1177/0165025410375922

Buss, K. A., & Kiel, E. J. (2013). Temperamental risk factors for pediatric anxiety disorders. In R. A. Vasa & A. K. Roy (Eds.), *Pediatric anxiety disorders: A clinical guide* (pp. 47–68). Springer. https://doi.org/10.1007/978-1-4614-6599-7_3

Dadds, M. R., & Tully, L. A. (2019). What is it to discipline a child: What should it be? A reanalysis of time-out from the perspective of child mental health, attachment, and trauma. *American Psychologist*, *74*(7), 794–808. https://doi.org/10.1037/amp0000449

Degnan, K. A., Henderson, H. A., Fox, N. A., & Rubin, K. H. (2008). Predicting social wariness in middle childhood: The moderating roles of child care history, maternal personality and maternal behavior. *Social Development*, *17*, 471–487. https://doi.org/10.1111/j.1467-9507.2007.00437.x

Dimidjian, S., Martell, C. R., Addis, M. E., Herman-Dunn, R., & Barlow, D. H. (2008). Behavioral activation for depression. In D. H. Barlow (Ed.), *Clinical handbook of psychological disorders: A step-by-step treatment manual* (4th ed., pp. 328–364). Guilford Press.

Eisenberg, N., Valiente, C., Spinrad, T. L., Cumberland, A., Liew, J., Reiser, M., Zhou, Q., & Losoya, S. H. (2009). Longitudinal relations of children's effortful control, impulsivity, and negative emotionality to their externalizing, internalizing, and co-occurring behavior problems. *Developmental Psychology*, *45*, 988–1008. https://doi.org/10.1037/a0016213

Ellis, L. K., & Rothbart, M. K. (2001, April). *Early Adolescent Temperament Questionnaire—Revised, Short Form*. Poster presented at the Biennial Meeting of the Society for Research in Child Development, Minneapolis, MN, USA. http://education-webfiles.s3-website-us-west-2.amazonaws.com/childcare/pdf/instrumental_docs/Early%20Adolescent%20Temperament%20Q-Revised%20Adolescent%20Short%20Form%20ID.pdf

Fox, N. A. (1994). Dynamic cerebral processes underlying emotion regulation. *Monographs of the Society for Research in Child Development*, *59*(2–3), 152–166. https://doi.org/10.1111/j.1540-5834.1994.tb01282.x

Fox, N. A., & Pine, D. S. (2012). Temperament and the emergence of anxiety disorders. *Journal of the American Academy of Child & Adolescent Psychiatry*, *51*(2), 125–128. https://doi.org/10.1016/j.jaac.2011.10.006

Fox, N. A., Rubin, K. H., Calkins, S. D., Marshall, T. R., Coplan, R. J., Porges, S. W., Long, J. M., & Stewart, S. (1995, December). Frontal activation asymmetry and social competence at four years of age. *Child Dev*, *66*(6), 1770–1784. PMID: 8556898.

Gartstein, M. A. (2021). Development and validation of the Mindful Parenting in Infancy Scale (MPIS). *Infancy*, *26*(5), 705–723. https://doi.org/10.1111/infa.12417

Gartstein, M. A., Hancock, G. R., Potapova, N., Calkins, S. D., & Bell, M. A. (2019). Electrophysiology of approach/avoidance: Development of the frontal EEG asymmetry. *Developmental Science*, e12891. https://doi.org/10.1111/desc.12891

Gatzke-Kopp, L. M., Willner, C. J., Jetha, M. K., Abenavoli, R. M., DuPuis, D., & Segalowitz, S. J. (2015). How does reactivity to frustrative non-reward increase risk for externalizing symptoms? *International Journal of Psychophysiology*, *98*(2), 300–309. https://doi.org/10.1016/j.ijpsycho.2015.04.018

Gray, J. A. (1994). Three fundamental emotion systems. In P. Edman & R. J. Davidson (Eds.), *The nature of emotion: Fundamental questions* (pp. 243–247). Oxford University Press.

Kagan, J., & Snidman, N. (2009). *The long shadow of temperament*. Harvard University Press.

Kiff, C. J., Lengua, L. J., & Zalewski, M. (2011). Nature and nurturing: Parenting in the context of child temperament. *Clinical Child and Family Psychology Review*, *14*(3), 251–301. https://doi.org/10.1007/s10567-011-0093-4

Kochanska, G. (1993). Toward a synthesis of parental socialization and child temperament in early development of conscience. *Child Development*, *64*(2), 325–347. https://doi.org/10.2307/1131254

Kochanska, G., & Knaack, A. (2003). Effortful control as a personality characteristic of young children: Antecedents, correlates, and consequences. *Journal of Personality*, *71*(6), 1087–1112. https://doi.org/10.1111/1467-6494.7106008

Lecavalier, L., Bodfish, J., Harrop, C., Whitten, A., Jones, D., Pritchett, J., Faldowski, R., & Boyd, B. (2020). Development of the Behavioral Inflexibility Scale for children with autism spectrum disorder and other developmental disabilities. *Autism Research*, *13*(3), 489–499. https://doi.org/10.1002/aur.2257

Lengua, L. J. (2015). *Social, emotional and academic competence for children and parents*. Center for Child & Family Well-Being, University of Washington. https://ccfwb.uw.edu/seacap/

Lengua, L. J., & Wachs, T. D. (2012). Temperament and risk: Resilient and vulnerable responses to adversity. In M. Zentner & R. Shiner (Eds.), *The handbook of temperament* (pp. 519–540). Guilford Press.

Linehan, M. M. (2015). *DBT® skills training manual* (2nd ed.). Guilford Press.

McMahon, R. J., & Forehand, R. L. (2003). *Helping the noncompliant child: Family-based treatment for oppositional behavior* (2nd ed.). Guilford Press.

Neff, K. (2023, October 24). *Self-compassion guided practices and exercise*. https://self-compassion.org/category/exercises/#exercises

Rothbart, M. K. (2007). Temperament, development, and personality. *Current Directions in Psychological Science*, *16*(4), 207–212. https://doi.org/10.1111/j.1467-8721.2007.00505.x

Rothbart, M. K., Ahadi, S. A., Hershey, K. L., & Fisher, P. (2001). Investigations of temperament at three to seven years: The Children's Behavior Questionnaire. *Child Development*, *72*(5), 1394–1408. https://doi.org/10.1111/1467-8624.00355

Rothbart, M. K., & Bates, J. E. (2006). Temperament. In N. Eisenberg, W. Damon, & R. M. Lerner (Eds.), *Handbook of child psychology: Vol. 3. Social, emotional, and personality development* (6th ed., pp. 99–166). Wiley.

Shimomaeda, L., Thompson, S. F., & Lengua, L. J. (2023). Differential effects of parental control on preschool-age adjustment depending on child effortful control. *Social Development*, 32, 1262–1279. https://doi.org/10.1111/sode.12692

Smith, C. L., & Bell, M. A. (2010). Stability in infant frontal asymmetry as a predictor of toddlerhood internalizing and externalizing behaviors. *Developmental Psychobiology*, *52*(2), 158–167. https://doi.org/10.1002/dev.20427

Teleki, J. K., Powell, J. A., & Dodder, R. A. (1982). Factor analysis of reports of parental behavior by children living in divorced and married families. *The Journal of Psychology*, *112*(2), 295–302. https://doi.org/10.1080/00223980.1982.9915387

Thomas, A., & Chess, S. (1977). *Temperament and development*. Brunner/Mazel.

INDEX

ABOUT THE AUTHORS

Liliana J. Lengua, PhD, is Maritz Professor of Psychology at the University of Washington, Director of the Center for Child and Family Well-Being, a child clinical psychologist, and mother of three children. She studies the effects of stress and adversity on children, examining risk and protective factors that contribute to children's resilience or vulnerability. She examines children's physiological stress responses, temperament, coping, parenting, parent mental health, and family contexts as risk and protective factors that account for the effects of adversity on children's social, emotional, and behavioral well-being. She has been an investigator on several federally funded projects and has developed mindfulness-based well-being programs for parents with infant- and preschool-age children, youth, and providers who work children and families. Dr. Lengua is the author of over 150 published papers and enjoys sharing her research and personal experiences in workshops with parents. Learn more about her work at https://ccfwb.uw.edu/ and visit https://www.psychologytoday.com/us/contributors/liliana-j-lengua-phd to check out her posts on *Psychology Today*.

Maria (Masha) Gartstein, PhD, is Professor of Psychology and Director of the Clinical Psychology Doctoral Program at Washington State University (WSU). Born in Moscow, Russia, she fully expected to spend the rest of her life there until her family immigrated to the United States. This transition contributed to Dr. Gartstein's appreciation of individual differences and the importance of context in shaping development, motivating her to pursue a PhD in clinical psychology. Her research has focused on psychological adjustment in the context of pediatric chronic illness, symptoms/disorders in childhood and adolescence, parent/family-oriented interventions, and the role of culture in temperament development. Chief among these themes is the role parenting plays in how temperament develops in early childhood, contributing to risk or protection with respect to later mental health. Dr. Gartstein continues to focus on the intersection of temperament and parenting, considering how early interaction dynamics influence brain activation underlying reactivity and regulation, studying changes across infancy. She has also been a provider of mental health services to children and families in a medical center context and community practice, and she currently supervises clinical psychology doctoral students at WSU in their assessment and therapy work. Learn more about Dr. Gartstein's work at https://labs.wsu.edu/infant-temperament/ and follow her @mashagartstein.